Collecting Lessons
David Hartman

Copyright 2007 by Wellness Press

Published by:

Wellness Press
The Wellness Institute
3716 - 274th Ave SE
Issaquah, WA 98029
800-326-4418
www.wellness-institute.org

ISBN 978-0-9622728-5-1

The dream was always running ahead of me. To catch up, to live for a moment in unison with it, that was the miracle.

Anais Nin

Ancient wisdom can be transmitted from masters of one age to students in another through dreams and visions called "mind-treasures." Mind treasures are teachings found in consciousness rather than sacred objects or texts in the physical world. Open yourself to the treasures herein, deposited long ago for the benefit of the future age in which they have now been found. Enjoy the adventure of discovering these buried treasures!

Table of Contents

Chapter One
Lessons of the Owl

If you want to wear a robe of spiritual sovereignty,
let your eyes weep with the wanting.

You that come to birth and bring the mysteries,
your voice-thunder makes us very happy.

Roar, lion of the heart,
and tear me open![1]

I was about to embark on a vision quest, my second one. The first had been three years earlier, and I had met mountain elk in the dark of a cold night. I was conferred that name some years earlier by a Native American teacher, but I had never heard the eerie soul-piercing call of an elk. When I did, I was both attracted to its ghostly nature and frightened by it. The single blanket I had with me in my grave-size space was thin protection from the cold. The night's bitter cold was periodically accentuated by the shivers of recognition of the haunting elk's call. My basic trust in life, although severely challenged, was my only protection from that threat.

I did not understand then how one collects lessons from such experiences, lessons that have been deposited for safekeeping by those who have gone before. I was about to discover, with eyes wide awake, just how powerfully these lessons can be delivered. And rather than being stored for future discovery in arcane books, or in treasure chests in caves, these lessons are stored in visions, dreams, in the experience of sacraments and rituals, in the hard-to-reach altered states encountered by those who yearn for and search for answers to the deepest existential questions.[2]

The Native American tradition of "crying for a vision" (*hanblecheyapi*) is also called "lamenting." Having prepared with the guidance of an elder, a teacher, one goes up on the mountain to pray and commune with the Creator. There are many reasons for going up to the mountaintop to lament. Perhaps the most important reason is to realize our oneness with all things, to know that all things are our relatives, and to seek knowledge of the Creator.[3] A vision is most likely to come to one whose motives are pure, and who seeks a vision that will bring strength and health to the people, the whole community. It is said that humans have two legs like the birds because, just as birds fly, humans can soar in spirit.

I had approached the *wichasha waken* (holy man) asking for help in going up on the mountain to lament and cry for a vision. We had prayed together, smoking the pipe and asking *Wakan-Tanka* (the Creator) to receive the prayers. I had made the tobacco prayer ties with which to surround my space, and now the time had come to go out. The *wichasha waken* prayed, "Grandfather, *Wakan-Tanka*, you are the first and always have been! Everything belongs to You, and to You we are sending a voice. This man wishes to offer his body to You. Upon the sacred Earth, our Mother and Grandmother, he will place his feet in a sacred manner.

"All the Powers of the world, the heavens and the star peoples, and the red and blue sacred days; all things that move in the universe, in the rivers, the brooks, the springs, all waters, all trees that stand, all the grasses of our Grandmother, all the sacred peoples of the universe: Listen! A sacred relationship with you all will be asked by this man, that his generations to come will increase and live in a holy manner."

This time my vision quest featured a different animal, the owl, and provided the lesson from the first vision quest much more explicitly. I was lead from the base camp, after one very hot round in the sweat lodge, out to my designated space in a large clearing surrounded by a thick forest of cedar and fir trees. Dusk was approaching, and I was somewhat preoccupied by the prospect of the encroaching chilly dark night. Scanning the trees around me that were now only unidentifiable shadows, I caught the image of an imposing black bird of prey sitting on a tree branch my height off the ground. I couldn't see the eyes, but I knew instinctively that they were staring at me. And I was feeling very intimidated.

After a few minutes of staring at each other, silent and unmoving, the owl flapped its mighty wings and flew deeper into the forest. My immediate inclination was to follow the owl, accepting what seemed to be its invitation. I would not physically leave my sacred space, made safe for me with prayer ties I had made which completely encircled it. But I had learned several months earlier how to spirit journey, separating my spirit body out from my physical body. In that body I could journey a few feet or thousands of miles away, and return. I considered using my spirit body to follow the owl wherever it was offering to lead me. But I was too uncertain of my ability to journey through the dark forest, and too suspicious of the owl's intention toward me. I chickened out and watched that great bird disappear, leaving behind an intact invitation to follow.

The Oglala Sioux shaman who had agreed to put me out on this vision quest had impressed me numerous times with the need to give the owl a wide berth. Owls were very powerful medicine, he said, too powerful for most people to contain. In fact, he said that he had only met one medicine person strong enough to "work with owl medicine," a Native woman in California. I was forewarned, and I was not just respectful of owls but really intimidated. I was scared to follow this black bird, and in fact I was very uncomfortable being in a "stare-down" with it.

Once the owl flew away, I made preparations to lie down and sleep for the night. However, I was not to sleep that night, nor for any of the coming four nights that I would be out. I was prepared to spend four days and nights on this vision quest without food or water, but I had not intended to do without sleep. I had a sleeping bag this time, and snuggled into it to keep warm and feel protected from the elements and the spirits. I didn't know who the spirits were, but my experience of them was almost tangible. I tossed and turned on the hard ground, unable to get comfortable, unable to sleep.

Tradition conveys that often the most powerful visions come during sleep, that these are not merely dreams but are much more real and powerful than dreams.[4]

In my drowsiness, I began to experience a group of people nearby, waiting for me to bring them books. It felt like a dream. I had a large supply of books, and somehow I knew which book to deliver to which person. Each individual had a specific need, and would benefit from a particular book. I took the appropriate book to one person after another, as if they had placed an order for it and I was providing it. Each person acknowledged the book with recognition, and expressed gratitude to me for bringing it to them. Soon I was distracted by the aches and pains of lying on the cold hard ground, and turned over from my left to right side. Immediately there were more people, waiting for their book. I tossed and turned all night, and with every new position I encountered more people waiting for a book. I questioned whether I was dreaming because it seemed like a dream. But there was no dreamless sleep in between these episodes. My experience was that of a dream, and not really a lucid dream. I got caught up with all these people and my interaction with them, and only got the sense of being in an alternate reality when I occasionally rolled over to get more comfortable physically. The alternate reality I assumed it to be was that of *dreams*. It was not until the last day of my vision quest that I had the startling realization that the alternate reality had in fact been that of *visions*.

That first night was long and arduous. I was relieved at the appearance of the first faint light of dawn, bringing an end to what I experienced as an ordeal. I stood and stretched, welcoming the daylight and the return of my "normal" state of consciousness. I enjoyed a quiet, leisurely day in my small sacred space, listening to the sounds of birds and squirrels, watching the patterns of shadows in the forest around me, and praying to the Creator for understanding. I catnapped for brief periods several times through that day, and anticipated sleeping well on my second night out. That did not happen.

My experience on the second night was similar to that of the first night, restlessly tossing and turning between episodes of working with multitudes of people. This time it was to give directions to people who were lost. The next two days followed the same pattern, the nights with no sleep and repetitious dreamlike encounters with multitudes of people in need of some form of assistance.

The fourth night's dreams were the most perplexing, surreal, and yet also the most detailed. I was on the security staff at an airport, watching people file past with their luggage, on the way to boarding a plane. They were embarking on a journey, but they all seemed uncertain about the procedure and the destination. They were confused. And the most striking feature of the experience was that I was just as confused as the embarking passengers. Elements of the scene seemed quite ridiculous. Terrorists looking like Groucho Marx rolled by "hidden" in luggage with large holes cut in the side, peeking out and flicking their cigar ashes. Most of the people moving through the line were just plain people who seemed perplexed about where they were and where they were going. I was charged with their security, and with providing them direction. Yet I was incompetent to do so because I was equally baffled and bewildered.

About mid-morning on the last day before being brought back in to the base camp, an owl came to sit in the very same location as the owl had been when I first entered my sacred space four days earlier. It was a brown spotted owl, smaller than the black one, and it seemed to be less threatening and more supportive. The owl's message was, "Be attentive! Stay conscious!" Under this owl's watchful gaze, the lesson came into sharp focus. We are called to assist one another at times of transition in life, transitions ranging from birth to death. And the quality of our service to others is limited by our own clarity. When others are cloudy with confusion, I must be transparently clear. When my experience is dreamlike, I must become lucid.

The *wichasha waken* greeted me silently when he came out to my sacred space to escort me on my return to base camp. Once we had purified ourselves in the sweat lodge, he spoke to me. "Each word that you said up on the mountain was heard, even by our Grandmother and Mother Earth. The coming generations will hear you. You left here four days ago. Tell me everything that happened to you up there, leaving nothing out." After I recounted my experiences of the four days, he said, "Oh, Grandfather, *Wakan-Tanka*, today you have helped us. You have been merciful to this man by giving him knowledge and a path which he may follow. You have made his people happy, and all the beings that move in the universe are rejoicing.

"Oh, *Wakan-Tanka*, You have established a relationship with this man, and through this relationship he will bring strength to his people. May this relationship exist until the very end!"

I had been provided boldly meaningful visions highlighting a profoundly fundamental truth, and yet my reaction had been irritation, seeing them as obstacles to getting sleep. I was beginning to understand how one can collect lessons deposited for safekeeping by those who have gone before, and also how I get in my own way.

What do we know about the state in which we are most likely to collect such lessons? I have found that the pivotal moments in the learning curve of personal development occur at the edge of ego disintegration, those moments when I stood on the precipice of uncertainty about the most basic assumptions in my life.[5] Approaching that edge occurs in one of two ways: either by the sudden, jarring imposition of an unexpected experience, an accident or a trauma; or by choosing a deintegration, which allows for some degree of preparation for the unexpected experience. Deintegration is a step backwards, an unlearning that penetrates self-delusion and brings a profound insight about a pattern of behavior that until that moment had been unconsciously habitual and unexamined. It seems to work best when the process is spiritually contained.

The significance of this experience, the lesson of the owls, gradually blossomed into certainty regarding a life path. Over the following two years, I began to realize that I needed to find ways of preparing myself to stay conscious and attentive during the transitional times, the dreamtime, the sleep time, and eventually the dying time. The two owls continued teaching me, long past my four days on the mountaintop. The black owl's lesson was clarity about the aspects of myself that would limit my development: the fear of becoming lost and of dying, the agitation of a restless mind, the heaviness of torpor and drowsiness that blunts awareness, and the mental laxity in which concentration has no strength.

The brown owl's lesson was "Be attentive! Stay conscious! When others are cloudy with confusion, I must be transparently clear. When my experience is dreamlike, I must become lucid."

These lessons would come to me again.

Chapter Two
Lessons about Separateness

At the verge of full fana *(annihilation in God) there seems to be a region of sweet confusion, the sense of being in many places at once saying multiple sentences. A hazy melting, fragile and nearly blank.*[6]

Within a year, a clarifying message came to me, at first in a book. The words stood out from the page I was reading like an image through binoculars. "We enter the bardo, the intermediate state after death, just as we enter dream after falling asleep. If our experience of dream lacks clarity and is of confused emotional states and habitual reactivity, we will have trained ourselves to experience the processes of death in the same way."[7] I could feel the threatening presence of the black owl, reminding me of his lesson. And on the same page, "Conversely, when we continually bring awareness to the immediate moment of experience, this capacity will soon be found in dream. As we cultivate presence in dream, we prepare ourselves for death." These words brought a visceral image of the brown owl, supporting me to move forward on the appointed path.

The juxtaposition of these two lessons first took me back to an experience of ten years earlier. I had been incorporating a "death rehearsal" into my spiritual practice for some months. I would occasionally allow the fantasy of impending death to come over me, and practice reacting to the threat with equanimity. This might come up during a plane trip, or a car ride, or a hike near a cliff. Sometimes the fantasy was of an intrusion of my home or some public place by a violent killer. I would create the experience of quietly accepting death, and using the brief moments of anticipation to connect with God in preparation. I had become quite good at making these pretenses seem realistic.

The experience, or more accurately *pseudo-experience*, was of a separation of my energy essence from this material vehicle, my body. I was rehearsing because I knew somehow that a conscious death could only happen when the time comes if I had already conquered any fear of death. Death is the glue that binds these bodies together and that can break them asunder,[8] and fear is the greatest enemy of advancement beyond *pseudo-experience*. Once I let go of fear, I can begin to truly receive those lessons of immortality; until then it is only empty pretense and no more. If I really experience disengaging from the physical *and being conscious* in that state, then what is there to be afraid of with death imminent?

I was in Mexico with my wife and some students, and playing with abandon on a deserted beach. The signs warned of potential riptides, but the surf seemed so quiet that afternoon. Suddenly I found myself under water, being sucked out to sea with a powerful undertow. I couldn't manage to get my head above water. I panicked. This momentary experience was unlike all the similar pretenses. I was desperate to get a breath of air, to live, to avoid dying.

I needed to have my spiritual egotism humbled, and would need to revisit that lesson many times. It is a constant battle between the self and the sense of self, between mindfulness and the restless mind, hazy torpor, and mental laxity.

That brush with death in the ocean so long ago was only a prelude to the vivid lesson I was to learn shortly. The owl would play its role again. But first I had to let owl come closer.

I had been pondering the meaning of my vision quest experience for a year. I knew intuitively that I must find a way to overcome my fear of the owl that had become so deeply imprinted within me. Until I could find the courage to follow him deep into the darkness of the unknown forest, and to accept his guidance, I was stuck at an impasse. The next step in making peace with owl came with my father's death. He was ninety-two years old, and his body was worn out. He was ready to leave this world, and his strong Christian faith allowed him to face death fearlessly. He was jovial and lucid on his last afternoon, with all of his family gathered around his hospital bed to recall and celebrate the important milestones in his life. We laughed and cried together, and prayed.

As nighttime approached, my father said goodbye to each son and daughter-in-law, and to each grandchild. Then, alone with my mother in the stillness of his last hours, he asked her to crawl in bed with him. They shared a profoundly silent commingling of souls, timeless tears of recognition, and, with no regrets, he took his last breath on this earth, and then his first in the life to come.

That very night I called a sweat lodge, and the same *wichasha waken* who had put me out on the mountain came to pour water for the people. About twenty men and women gathered around the fire which held the grandfather rocks. It was dusk, a magical time, and the holy man reverently dusted off each person in turn with an eagle feather and the smoke of burning sage. Midway around the circle, the shaman stopped and said quietly, "Listen. Do you hear the owl? He has come to honor a fallen warrior." We all listened intently as the owl, unseen in the dark trees nearby, serenaded us for several minutes. When Owl stopped calling, he did not fly away but stayed to maintain a vigil during our sacred sweat lodge ceremony. The *wichasha waken* completed saging the remaining people in the circle, and we entered the lodge for what turned out to be an intensely hot four rounds.

My father had been a warrior in his long life in many ways. He survived the Great Depression, World War II, losing an infant child, and innumerable battles to live in integrity and maintain dignity. Owl recognized him, and honored him. And, although I didn't realize it until my next encounter with Owl a year later, I recognized Owl that night as a potential ally. What I had experienced as a chilling sinister presence in my vision quest, was now morphing into a messenger demanding healthy respect but not necessarily fear.

That next encounter with Owl was in the dreamtime. I had been following a practice since my father's death of asking myself throughout the day, "Is my experience in this moment a dream, or is this real?" I knew this practice was prescribed by the traditions of Tibetan dream yoga,[9] those of Siberian shamans,[10] and by the western scientists who study lucid dreaming.[11] This quizzical musing had begun to inhabit the terrain of my daily life, popping up in moments of the banal as well as moments of wonder and awe. The practice was helping me to move past simply taking for granted the "reality" of everyday activities. And it was bringing more lucidity into my dreamtime activities.

One night, amidst restless sleep and an intangible sense of something ominous about to happen, I became aware of being in the clearing familiar to me from my vision quest. It was dusk, and the black owl was perched in a nearby tree. He and I were alone, and it seemed as if we were the only two life forms in existence. There was no one else. That fact made for an immediate sense of intimacy between us. I felt no fear or threat, and yet I also felt a great divide of difference between us. How could I communicate with Owl? What did I want from him, and what did I want to share with him? He seemed to be so alien from me, so very dissimilar.

Unlike the first night of my vision quest, the black owl did not fly away deeper into the forest. Owl did something totally unexpected. He stepped inside of me. The movement was almost instantaneous, and it was more bewildering than frightening. In that moment I experienced the two of us inhabiting one body, as if I could almost identify its essence in various parts of my body, and mine in other parts. Owl seemed to be located primarily in the lower part of my torso: in the groin, the belly, and the diaphragm. He was stretching, as if attempting to expand so as to fill the entire body.

Because I had become accustomed to asking myself the question, "Is my experience in this moment a dream, or is this real?" throughout the day, I suddenly became aware that I was dreaming. Or was I? The reality testing at the foundation of that question was just as perplexing to me as the experience of this owl inside me. And a fleeting thought crossed my mind here; I marveled that I was not afraid, and that I was not becoming enveloped in the quicksand of confusion and drowsiness. I felt more alert and conscious than perhaps I ever had in my life. And at the same time, I felt totally puzzled about what was going on.

Multiple layers of reality swirled around me. I was in the clearing from my vision quest. I was dreaming. I was alone in the world with this owl, and we were bumping into each other inside this body. Owl sent a message to me somehow, I didn't know how. It was an invitation to journey down into the depths of this physical body, into the bowels, to meet him there. I knew instinctively how to do that, and without hesitation I began to descend the windpipe, past the opening to the lungs and into the stomach. We were on an equal footing now, sharing the same place of power and insight. Of course we were, after all he had entered me. It was becoming difficult to differentiate between his essence and mine.

What is going on here? I was mystified. Then, communicating in the same silent but certain way as before, Owl revealed the meaning of my descent into the bowels of this body and into a boundaryless summit with him. The aspects of myself that limit my development were located in my head, not in my heart or in my guts. It was my restless mind that brought on torpor and drowsiness, not my body. My body could only be robbed of strength and vitality by the laxity of mental resolve. And at the root of all these forms of self-sabotage was the mistaken belief in separation, separateness. Seeing Owl in the tree from my place in the clearing, I had felt separate and judged him to be alien. When he entered me and invited me to meet in a place without boundaries, I let go of that sense of separateness. Knowing that I was dreaming, I nonetheless felt more lucid than ever before, loosening the distinction between awake time and dreamtime.

Gradually the ceaseless flow of thoughts did indeed cease. Time coalesced into the experience of a now unencumbered by past or future.

How long this state lasted I have no idea, but gradually I did return to "normal," realizing that I was lying in bed and "awakening from a dream." The twilight transition seemed timeless, and pregnant with the potential of a limitless future. I felt intimately connected with all the universe.

Owl had not taught me the lesson, but rather modeled it within a shared consciousness: clarity that the aspects of myself that would limit my development were fears, the agitation of a restless mind, the drowsiness that blunts awareness, and an inability to concentrate. What gratitude I experienced for this ally and guide, my friend Owl. And yet I did not feel separate from him, or from anything in my surroundings that morning. An awareness was growing at the periphery of my conscious perception that the descent into the bowels of my physical body was a descent also on another level, that the place of the boundaryless summit was a real place to which I could return. And an even dimmer realization was flickering that the descent to this place was somehow, inexplicably, a return to the womb.

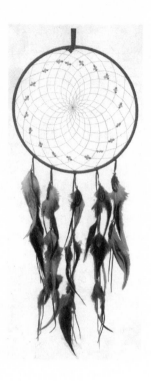

Chapter Three
Guardians at the Threshold

Jung said that soul moves at the weak point where the personality is thin, where things are not secure and stable. That's where soul has an entry.[12]

Every ascent to the heights is preceded by a descent. Those descents in my life have sometimes been gentle drops, but more often freefalls all the way to the depths. With hindsight I can see that each fall compelled me to find the path to a new ascent. And that path always provided challenges which strengthened me, carrying me to even higher levels.

I wanted to know more about the experience I had with Owl. What I was really attracted to was the experience of oneness, of my identity expanding beyond its normal well-defined limits. I continued to feel somewhat intimidated by Owl, because my associations were with death, and ghosts, and the dark. Maybe I could find a way to journey to the place of boundaryless summit without necessarily doing so with Owl. I began reading what I could find about journeys between worlds, but the immediacy of the journey into my body was receding quickly. Everyday life seemed to take over rapidly, like a jungle overgrowing a small, temporary clearing.

One day, I had a reminder, a "wake-up call" that I needed to get the machete out to reclaim that clearing. A bear came calling to my home. My wife had put up a bird feeder in front of the house, and initially I was annoyed because we were feeding squirrels more than birds. Soon enough, however, a big black mamma bear sauntered out of the forest and over to the bird feeder. She stood on her back legs and grabbed the container of seeds. She tore the block of suet, meant to feed woodpeckers, off its stand and casually sat down to eat. I was watching this bear from my living room window, feeling even more annoyed than I had been with the squirrels. I was angry, feeling taken advantage of. So, without thinking, I ran out the door waving my arms and yelling, "Shooo! Go away now!"

Bear did not flinch as she looked my way with a disdaining glance, and continued eating. I had not anticipated this response, or actually this lack of response. Suddenly I experienced the same chill of fear that I had in my vision quest space, with Owl seemingly challenging me so openly. Bear could easily lunge at me and maul me to death in an instant. And yet I didn't feel that she would, or even wanted to. What did she want?

Then something totally unexpected happened. I was suddenly overtaken with drowsiness, and could not stop myself from collapsing onto the ground with an overwhelming need to fall asleep. Some small part of me became aware of a momentary flash of apprehension, of the absurdity of succumbing to sleep in the midst of confrontation with a bear. Yet I couldn't help myself. I couldn't stay awake. I fell into a deep unconscious sleep, as if my time to hibernate had come, and it could not be denied.

I slumbered in a state of nonbeing, yet with a faint awareness of being. The only experience of "me" or of individual identity at all was a vague sense, through mist, and from a great distance. Vignettes of potential individual identities floated into focus, unbidden, and then dissolved.

I became aware of sitting in a circle with perhaps twenty other people, listening intently to each one sharing profoundly, intimately, openly. I had no personal identity, as if awakening with amnesia into an unknown life. And I "knew" these people in the same way that I knew myself: I knew nothing of their life circumstances or histories, yet I felt deeply connected to and trusting of each one. We seemed to be acting as a governing council, a council of elders, and at the same time to be studying, exploring, marveling at some vast overarching set of principles. I knew those principles in the same way that I knew myself and the others in the circle: I knew nothing of their structure or their content, yet I felt deeply connected to and trusting of them. The scene dissolved, as did my experience of personal identity. Again I basked in an indescribable state of nonbeing.

I became aware of meeting other beings in a similar space of reverie, of amnesia. Next there were cockroaches communicating their life experience to me telepathically. Giant sequoia trees shared their timeless sense of an eternal now. The bear roused herself from the same hibernation of nonbeing as I did, and assured me that the loss of a sense of personal identity carried with it the loss of a sense of separation from all creation. She insisted that it was time to reclaim that clearing in the jungle of everyday consciousness, cluttered as it was with distractions. And she was most explicit: the reclaiming was necessary daily, and was in fact the purpose of every night's deep sleep. Bear spoke to me of that faint awareness of being, of nonbeing really, that descended on me through the misty hibernation.

Gradually I became aware of myself lying on the ground next to the birdfeeder, apparently alone. Yet I felt connected to all the world as if tapping into a root system that we all shared: the insects and trees, the people and the bear. I resolved to keep this perspective and not let it recede so quickly into everyday life, to pull me back into my everyday perspective, the jungle so easily becoming overgrown again. Here I could see those self-limiting aspects of myself at work, the fears and agitation, torpor and mental laxity. They seemed like fierce guardians of my separateness and vulnerability. Now, however, they were beginning to appear in their true nature: guardians of initiation and preparation at the threshold of undreamed adventures.

Chapter Four
Escorting Souls of the Dead

The Lame Goat
You've seen a herd of goats
going down to the water.

The lame and dreamy goat
brings up the rear.

There are worried faces about that one,
but now they're laughing.

Because look, as they return,
that goat is leading!

There are many different kinds of knowing.
The lame goat's kind is a branch
that traces back to the roots of presence.

Learn from the lame goat,
and lead the herd home.[13]

Following this powerful dreamtime lesson, I returned to my everyday
life with a profoundly deep sense of inner quiet and peace. I continued to
ask myself the question throughout the day, and increasingly throughout
dreamtime, "Is my experience in this moment a dream, or is this real?" I
continued to function in my life's work and my relationships, yet the
unreality of that distinction spread more and more.

Now that I had let Owl and Bear come closer, dissolving the
separateness between us, apparently the time was approaching for me to
learn at a deeper, more visceral level the lesson first broached at the time
of my brush with death in the ocean so long ago.

We enter the state after death just as we enter dream after falling
asleep. The dream can seem to be a terrifying nightmare, or it can seem to
be an intoxicating paradise. And of course the question, "Is this a dream or
is it reality?" was more and more constant in my everyday perception.

One day I was tending the fire, heating up the stones for a ceremonial
sweat lodge. I sat near the blazing fire, entranced by its liveliness and
playfulness. The grove of Douglas Fir and Cedar trees surrounding the
lodge comforted me, and provided cover for many animal spirits, visible

and invisible. A gentle breeze quietly whistled through the clearing, and I heard these unformed and unspoken words: *Here wander many souls of the dead, each in need of direction.*[14] Who was speaking to me? Was it really addressed to me at all?

I began to feel just like I had when I fell into the hibernation state in the presence of Bear, into a state of nonbeing. Through the mist of timelessness, eventually I became aware of people. I "knew" these people in the same way as before, even though I knew nothing of their life circumstances or histories. Each one seemed to be confused and aimless, listlessly on a forgotten errand.[15] The scenario felt familiar to me, with the difference that I was not as confused as before. And yet I seemed to have less of a sense of personal identity at the same time. I knew these souls, I felt intimately connected to them. And I had a sense of the direction each was seeking.

My awareness of the wandering souls receded and I became aware again of the fire in the clearing, and the forest. Then the souls became foreground again. I was caught up in a netherworld, unable to intentionally navigate but content to be windblown through and between these two places. A very clear realization dawned on me: bringing these worlds together produced an immense gift to each. The direction sought by the wandering souls seemed to come more into focus for them with the presence of the ceremonial fire. And the sweat lodge ceremonial grounds seemed to become activated, more vibrantly alive, with the presence of these souls.

Where was Owl? Where was Bear? Where was Mountain Elk? None were needed, apparently. The fire provided consciousness, the forest containment. These souls' problem was illusory, and the repair, their clarity, was provided like manna from heaven.

What happened next is completely inexplicable. I decided to feed the fire, and reaching into the stack of firewood, I found two old crumpled pieces of paper. I glanced at them before burning them, and immediately a chill went up my spine. A message was written on the papers, one that I did not understand but that was somehow deeply disturbing to me.

To anyone who finds this message
          For God's sake take heed
We are here alone and cut off
                    where is here? We don't know
          who we are and why
                    we can go no further is plain . . .

Damn! how could we be so stupid
          we shouldn't have let the others out of our sight
There are only two of us now
                    and everything seems crooked
                         like a picture on a wall awry
          There is nothing to judge it by: freefall . . .

He is jealous of my powers in magic
          and I suspect his aloofness
                    we are becoming irrational
          Neither of us can trust the other with the Treasure . . .

All sense of time is lost
          I remember nothing from before this experience
And yet I fight off all thoughts of the future
                    for surely only despair awaits us both . . .

At least I take heart that someday
          someone will find this and understand
                              our horror
          If you have reached this point
you know everything
               we know and so there is nothing
          I can tell you that could help
                    May God take pity on you . . .

I have slept for a long time, restlessly
          he hides from me always
                    and neither one of us dares to
                         touch the Treasure . . .

But before I slept I experienced
a curious sensation
For a few moments I felt that this too
this horror and despair
is another live Pathway
perhaps even necessary
and that it is still not the end of our search . . .

Our mutual jealousy forces us to an
awareness of the Treasure
at all possible moments
It is becoming difficult to think
about anything else . . .

I rack my brains to find a way
out of this dilemma
For if our future depends on he and I alone
I fear we are doomed
and nothing can be done without . . .

The Treasure is a great burden I am forced to watch it
constantly
and I grow exceedingly tired . . .

I am going mad
I actually don't know any more
what is impossible
only that all I have learned is untrue
and that I remain impotent . . .

I am alone and
haven't seen him
my music is a distant roar - of my inner ear?
My conversation consists of reverberating echoes
and my mind is
coming unglued
unglued from what?

I cannot move
not because of walls, not due to curtains
but because there is nowhere to go
nowhere to go
now here

How had these papers and their message come to me? Why? What I did not know at that time was that other messages would find me in equally mysterious ways along the journey that lay ahead.

Chapter Five
More Souls, but They're Not Dead

According to traditional Irish wisdom, there is a plane of being somewhere between life and death; called the "thin place," it is that place in time where the reality of this existence overlaps and intermingles with the reality of the existence beyond it.[16]

I was not really used to contact with these lost and wandering souls, but it did not surprise or mystify me any more, either. I seemed to encounter them at times not of my choosing, and yet I was more and more prepared to work with them when asked to. However, I now began to discover that not all of the souls that crossed my path were dead. Inexplicably, some of the souls I encountered were in a different sort of lost state: rather than being preoccupied with a forgotten errand or mission, they seemed to be frozen in a state of suspended animation. With the dead souls I had become familiar with, I knew them without any personal identity or history. But with these undead souls I could not help but know their history in detail. The reason is that they seemed to be suspended in a specific experience from their past, always a terrible and traumatic one.

One day I encountered the soul of a six-year-old girl, sitting absently in a corner of her bedroom, disconnected from her body and her incestuous father's attentions. The girl's disembodied life was lifeless, fragmented, paralyzed. And the scene clearly happened decades earlier: the soul I stumbled upon was frozen in time.[17] The woman that the girl had become did not even know she was missing a vital part of herself. These souls presented me with a daunting challenge: it was not a departing soul in need of direction, but rather the still alive person in need of reconnection with herself.

How could I help reunite the little-girl soul with the woman? The six-year-old didn't know she existed, and the woman didn't know she was missing. In this time and place I seemed to have an "objective" view of the woman's lifespan, unlike with the departed souls who seemed to have no history. The six-year-old and the woman existed in one frozen moment in time, not separated by decades of elapsed time, yet more profoundly disconnected from each other than if they were. In fact, I began to see other aspects of this woman's lifespan, tableaus of lifeless, fragmented, paralyzed girls of various ages. One was a twelve-year-old girl sexually assaulted by a friend of her father's. She sat staring out her bedroom window at nothing, oblivious to the betrayal of her body-self in the room. Another was a fourteen-year-old girl runaway, numbly going through the motions of providing oral sex to a man in return for a meal and a pack of cigarettes.

These tableaus flickered by, almost like a series of drawings fanned rapidly enough to simulate motion. I could see the pattern of experiences in this woman's life, and the increasingly diminished remnant of her original self as she left pieces behind with each wound.

I began to see other undead soul fragments. These were the remnants of what had once been in people's lives. The child's mythic imagination, profound sense of wonder, and capacity for innocent enchantment with magic – where does that go, what happens to them when the child grows up to become reasonable and rational? We know they do not just disappear into nonexistence. They emerge when consciousness takes a vacation, in our fantasies and dreams. I began to see these sprites as the neglected children they really were. I could see their history, and these undead were suspended in a specific experience, too, not a traumatic one but a neglected one. This child was locked away in a dark corner, out of sight, allowed to wither away, autistic, deprived of the lifeblood of activation.[18]

I was helpless to do anything to help the people around me shadowed by their own undead child souls. And they were helpless to even comprehend their predicament. Clearly, I needed help if I had any hope of intervening effectively on their behalf. And suddenly a thought darted into my mind: despite the differences between these dead-but-not-dead souls and the wandering departed souls, perhaps they might share the capacity to be contacted through ceremony, such as the sweat lodge. The fire that I sometimes tended to heat the grandfather stones, in the clearing in the forest, with all the spirits nearby, perhaps that fire could help reunite these people with their lost, abandoned, psychically dead former selves. Do we not all long for that?

Chapter Six
Deeper into the Body

All the soarings of my mind begin in my blood.[19]

The memory of Owl stepping inside of me that one dreamtime, into the lower part of my torso, had faded out of conscious recollection. Until another similar experience came upon me, that is. I felt angry about something that happened during the day, one of those inconsequential triggering events that surprised me with its ability to call up such intense feeling. I felt the anger burning deep within, and rising up toward my throat where it could find expression. I could feel the energy in my belly, rising up through the windpipe, and then suddenly I was not angry. What a strange surprise.

The anger dissipated because I became preoccupied, fascinated with the inner workings of my lower abdomen, my stomach, intestines and liver. I experienced a surreal transparency to my body, seeing the organs at work as if observing the interlocking gears of a precise timepiece. The focus seemed to be on my liver. It was noticeably the largest organ, and it contained the most blood. It was dark, impenetrable. It was the Under World, the World of Power!

And sitting in my liver, staring at me as if to say, "Who else might you find here?" was Owl. He carefully explained that the liver is indeed doorway to the Under World, origin of the darkest passions, particularly the bloody, smoky ones of wrath, jealousy, lust and greed.[20] The most archaic animal impulses spark to life here. They may appear unbidden, as if appearing out of nowhere, yet I could see in my transparent view that they were actually vestiges of the unburied dead, hauntingly lingering at the threshold between the netherworld and my physical reality. Just as I had been allowed to see the wandering souls of the dead in the forest clearing by the sweat lodge fire, I could see these primal emotions materializing. Instead of souls wandering the forest in need of direction, these were fragments of unlived life still longing to live.

Rage propelled them out of their confinement in the shadows, seeking expression, demanding satisfaction. But they were not tamed upon entering physical reality out of the shadows. They were not wandering meekly, aimlessly, like the other unburied dead I had encountered. These primitive fragments of unlived life exploded through the threshold, blowing disdainfully past the guardians. And in that moment I realized that the fear

I had always held for Owl was actually fear of that which emerges from the bloody, smoky Under World, the hellish shadow realm, fetid breeding ground of unlived life.

Another set of primal emotions also materialize here, entering the body from the netherworld. However this other set of emotions is vastly different from those already mentioned. These are feelings of terror and shame, blame and self-pity, grief, suffering and depression, the very aspects of self that would limit one's development: the fear of becoming lost and of dying, the agitation of a restless mind, the heaviness of torpor and drowsiness that blunts awareness, and the mental laxity in which concentration has no strength. These are the energies of unlived life which have succumbed to the pull of death, more fearful of the return of the repressed even than of annihilation.

Through the transparency of my body I could easily see these two primeval forces being carried through the nervous system. Wrath, jealousy, lust and greed, focused on the subject of their obsession, surged through the sympathetic branch. And fear, shame, blame, self-pity, and grief, consumed with introspect, seeped through the parasympathetic branch. My body looked to me like a surreal schematic drawing in a medical textbook. This is called the autonomic nervous system because it runs automatically, without conscious control. Now I could see clearly the *un*conscious control: the fragments that psychologists call autonomous complexes. With a shiver a statement came into my mind that I had read long ago, and was only now really beginning to comprehend: *Everyone knows that people have complexes, but what is not so well known ... is that complexes can have us.*[21] These were the Spirit of obsession and attachment to life, and the Spirit of destruction and detachment from life, and they can so easily cast a spell on the rational mind.

In some mysterious way I knew that Owl could not show me the solution to this dilemma, but that someone could, and eventually would.

Two dawning insights began to slowly materialize. One, that just as the lotus flower, that most delicate of blossoms, grows up from the deep mud of the lake bottom, so too only from the depths of the Under World can sufficient passion for life and growth come to fuel the drive for spiritual attainment. And secondly, again, a dim realization was flickering at the periphery of my conscious perception that the descent to this place was somehow, inexplicably, a return to the womb.

Chapter Seven
The Sun and the Moon

Say the body is like this lamp.
It has to have a wick and oil. Sleep and food.
If it doesn't get those, it will die,
And it's always burning those up, trying to die.

But where is the sun in this comparison?
It rises, and the lamp's light
Mixes with the day.[22]

The vivid image of the lotus flower stayed with me for several days, growing in luminous significance. The contrast is stark between the dark, primordial mud from which its roots grow up through the swampy waters and the breathtakingly beautiful blossom floating gently on the rippling surface. These, too, are the energies of the moon and the sun. The one is cool, dark, feminine, fertile, the reflected light of the unconscious. The other is the blazing red hot of action and vibration, masculine, the radiance of self-consciousness.

These days were filled with recognition of this polarity at every turn. As soon as I became aware of a boisterous group of boys on the street corner, I noticed a quiet old man sitting on a bench at the bus stop, observing them serenely. Standing in line at the grocery store, I marveled at the contrast between two women: one was highly agitated, talking on her cell phone with a doctor's office demanding an immediate appointment, and the other was animated, absorbed in playing a word game with her pre-school daughter. I kept seeing the sun and the moon everywhere, and it was becoming obvious to me that in either case the individual was unconscious, under the spell of Spirits. These powers would come and go as they please so that at some unpredictable time the second woman might begin to act like the first.

One morning began with bright sunshine streaming into my kitchen, illuminating the leaves on the trees outside the window as well as the room inside. I felt uplifted, a glowing sense of optimism filling my outlook. I became aware of an actual physical sensation of buoyancy in my heart and abdomen. "Life is good," I said to myself. I had work to do, and set about it with enthusiasm. By midmorning dark rain clouds rolled in and within a few minutes they had chased the sunshine into hiding. My cheerfulness dissipated within minutes as well, replaced by a growing sense of gloom and discouragement. The change in me, like the change in the weather, seemed to occur suddenly and arbitrarily. I was not even aware of the change in me. And as if appearing out of nowhere came to me a thought: *depression, elation, sadness and playfulness, all nothing more than the changing weather of the mind.*[23] The emotions that come and go, can they really be as arbitrary as the sudden rain storm? And is it possible to find the perspective of the weatherman who sees and reports on the changing weather without actually being affected by it. Rain or shine, the weatherman is in a climate-controlled studio observing all the changes outside. Where is that studio and who is that weatherman?

I was soon to find the guidance that Owl could not show me regarding how to navigate the polarities. I had become absorbed in my observations of sun and moon, to the exclusion of the question "Is my experience in this moment a dream, or is this real?" And perhaps for this reason the vision that came upon me one evening was at first jarringly disorienting. I was sitting in my library, a small intimate room with books covering not only every inch of shelf space but piled up on every tabletop. It felt like a warm inviting cave to me, comforting, private, and introspective. Whether I literally fell asleep or not I do not know, but the next thing I knew I was sitting quietly with Bear. We were in a cramped dark place, and I was overwhelmed with the sensation of her soft breath, slow and even. There was something almost hypnotic about the cadence of that breath. And yet I was disturbed about being curled up with Bear in this closed space, close enough to touch her coarse hair.

Despite our proximity, Bear seemed to be far away, preoccupied with distant visions and an ancient silent purpose. I could sense fragments of communication filtering out toward me from Bear's reverie. *This place is Dream Lodge.* Then silence again. I began relaxing more now that I experienced contact with Bear, and trusted that she represented no threat to me. *We enter this womb-cave to digest the year's experience.* Silence returned. Bear's rhythmic breathing again entranced me, bringing a reassuring sense of balance and security. I felt as though a comforting blanket of order and coherence was descending over my whole body, my emotions and my thoughts. I had a brief glimpse of that transparent medical textbook drawing of my body, and I could sense that the nervous system was settling down, the lymph and hormonal systems were entering into a peaceful rhythm with the breath and with the heartbeat.

I was now beginning to understand more fully the experience I had when Bear came calling at my house those several years before, when I had slumbered in a state of nonbeing, yet with a faint awareness of being. The only experience of "me" or of individual identity at all was a vague sense, through mist, and from a great distance. Now I was observing Bear engaged in that same hibernation state. At that earlier time, I had an awareness of sitting in a circle with others, seemingly a council of elders. Now I began to re-experience the same phenomenon, realizing that the others were my ancestors here to broaden my perspective. The harder I tried to focus my attention on them in order to learn what they offered to teach me, the hazier my comprehension became. *Enter the silence and know.* Bear's quiet suggestion barely drifted across the intimate space between us. She was far away, and yet I felt a deep connection growing between us.

I surrendered to the entrancing breathing pattern again, slow and even, unhurried yet purposeful. My heartbeat willingly fell into synch with my breath. Clearly, the breath was the key to balancing all the body's systems, bringing harmony to the polarities inherent in each one. The call and response of the nervous system seemed to be working in accord, as a team of two disciplined horses pulling a wagon effortlessly. *We are sitting in the West, the place of intuition, the right brain.* I saw a map of my head that Bear was somehow projecting for me to see. The South was in the direction of my forehead, and the North in the direction of the back of my head. The right brain lay in the West, and the left brain in the East.[24] I felt as though this map provided an important key to understanding the specialized functions of different parts of the brain, but I could not make sense of it yet.

Quiet as Bear's thoughts were, their clarity struck me like a bolt of lightning. The synchronized breath and heartbeat activate the receptive right brain functions that allow conscious control of the body's autonomic responses. This was the answer to the dilemma of those fragments of unlived life propelled out of their confinement in the shadows by their longing to live. The unburied dead deserved a thoughtful burial. And that was Bear's meaning in saying that the purpose of entering the cave was to digest the year's experience, to process what was now past and arrive at completion with it. To leave no unfinished business that could fester and grow into something that might take on a life of its own.

But what did she mean by *womb-cave*? I was just too tired to pursue that thought. I had been struggling to stay mentally alert enough to understand this experience with Bear, and now my strength was sapped entirely. I gave way to the deepest sleep I have ever entered, and awoke the next morning curled up on the floor of my library, reflective and humbly appreciative for the blessing of the Dream Lodge. Although I probably could not articulate it, I felt a profound inner knowing about the place of coherent cooperation between the Sun and the Moon.

Chapter Eight
Mind Treasures

The question one must ask above all with any neurosis is not, "How do we eliminate it," but rather, "Whither does it want to go?" [25]

This Mind treasure, hidden by some ancient master or perhaps by one of my ancestors, came to me in a visionary experience, or maybe it was a dream. Only a few days after the Dream Lodge experience, I happened to be sitting on a swing on my porch, reflecting on that experience. One particular fragment dominated my memory: the circle of elders that I sat in which seemed to be offering me lessons. I should have paid more attention to them, I told myself. I missed a golden opportunity, once more, by being too confused and unclear. It turned out that their teaching would reach out to me in a different, highly unexpected way. And this time no animal Spirits were involved.

It was a warm lazy summer day as I sat on my porch, and I gradually fell into a deep sleep. At some point in (or rather out of) time, my entire being and all my attention became focused on an idea. It felt like I was in a dream, except that there wasn't any sensual content to the experience. That is, I didn't see or hear anything. The whole of my experience was contained in this concept: *When we're unaware of how we constrict our energy, we perpetuate our own entrapment.* [26] The utter simplicity of that concept grabbed me and seemed to almost shake me. In fact, I awakened with a startle, surprised to find myself sitting on that swing on my porch. I had to adjust my perspective, as if I was entering a brightly lit area from a dark space, squinting to keep from closing my eyes.

I knew that the idea was centrally related to the experience in the Dream Lodge with Bear, and to the unlived lives emerging from the Under World through the liver. But I could not immediately see in what way. At first what seemed most obvious to me was the contrast between my image of constriction and the image of the unburied dead exploding out of their confinement in the shadows, demanding satisfaction. Then a fleeting thought emerged, only partially formed and misty, that constriction had caused the confinement in the first place. Unburied and still longing for life, the not-yet dead are trapped in the netherworld. Movement forward into life and expression is denied, but so is movement away from life to a quiet resting place. Trapped by ignorance in limitation and inertia. [27]

Who would help me understand these things? Later that same day the answer came, and I was certain that it came from that unknown circle of elders. After the episode on the porch, I felt the need for rest, and had walked out to the sweat lodge clearing, a quiet space to sit in. Even without the fire and the ceremony, the space seemed to elicit a contemplative state of mind. My eyes were open yet unfocused, taking in the surrounding forest. I usually sensed the presence of spirits here, and felt comforted by them. My thoughts drifted and became less structured. I guess you would call it a state of reverie. After some time, I began to feel that I was not alone. The presence I sensed was soft, nurturing, and human. Just as before, on the porch swing, I didn't see or hear anything, yet I felt as though I was being wrapped gently in a warm blanket of wisdom: *The first stage of spiritual unfoldment is the conscious recognition of bondage. Until they irk us, we can make no real effort to strike off our chains.*[28] Unlike the previous experience, however, I did not awaken with a startle. I lapsed easily into a quiet restful sleep, secure in knowing that, for whatever reason, trustworthy and knowledgeable elders were willing to teach me. And they knew how to establish contact.

I did not understand that means of contact at the time, and only later learned about the centuries-old Tibetan tradition, the transmission of ancient wisdom through dreams and visions called "mind-treasure" (*gong-gter*). Mind treasures are found in consciousness rather than in the physical world. The tradition holds that masters of one age hide *terma* (sacred objects, texts and teachings) for the benefit of the future age in which they are found. *Terma* may be found in physical locations; in the elements of water, wood, earth, or space; or received in dreams, visionary experience, and found directly in deep levels of consciousness. How fortunate I was to have stumbled across a place of access to these buried treasures.[29]

The mystery of those pieces of parchment I had found in the woodpile was now disentangling. It was another way for ancient wisdom to be conveyed. And the veiled message in its obscure epic poem was becoming much more clear. My focus needed to be on becoming consciously aware of my bondage.

Chapter Nine
Mountain Elk's Message

Realization does not arise out of words.
Understanding does not come from mere suggestions.
I urge all those who work for Enlightenment
To meditate with perseverance and effort.
Endurance and effort overcome the greatest of difficulties.
May there be no obstacles for those who seek Enlightenment.[30]

I was thinking so hard about these things that my head hurt. What had begun as a pleasant interlude on my porch wound up a confusing attempt to unravel the message that had been revealed to me. I wanted distraction, yet I also felt that I was at a point on my path close to reaching a summit, that just a little more work and I'd be standing at a zenith with a panoramic view of what lay behind and ahead. At the same time, I could not forget the foreboding warnings about needing to be conscious of my bondage to limitations and ignorance.

You have more stamina than you know; forego the quick and easy for the long and steady. You have already hit your stride before becoming aware of it. Mountain Elk conveyed immense encouragement to keep going, just when I needed it most. I vowed to myself that I would find a way to remember his message at future times of greatest need.

Chapter Ten
The Fallacy of Separateness

At times I feel as if I am spread out over the landscape and inside things, and am myself living in every tree, in the splashing of the waves, in the clouds and the animals that come and go, in the procession of the seasons.[31]

Despite my dogged determination, or perhaps because of it, I found myself in a curious period of time that seemed timeless but was actually about two weeks. Mysterious interludes of reverie would occur in the midst of my everyday activities. Standing in the checkout line at the grocery store, I slipped away to an experience in a forest clearing much like the one I maintained for our sweat lodge. There were several animals there that were at first oblivious to my presence. Then, taking notice of me, they moved toward me with curiosity and a sense that I might be helpful to them. There was a mouse, a turtle, and an antelope. The mouse offered its advice to me: *I touch everything with my whiskers in order to know it. See what is up close; pay attention to the seemingly insignificant.* And what he wanted from me was to raise him up so he could see the Sacred Mountain in the distance. The turtle suggested: *You carry a shield to protect you, like my shell. What others think of you is none of your business; go inside yourself and honor your own experience.* What turtle wanted from me was to be mindful of the cycle of give and take, to give back to the earth as she has given to me. The antelope told me: *I live fully aware of the ever-present possibility of death. Be aware of your mortality, and truly live. Take decisive action now.* Antelope wanted from me to take no more than needed. And I suddenly returned to the grocery store when the clerk asked me, "Paper or plastic?"

The juxtaposition of that forest meadow and the grocery store was so great that I shook my head in disbelief and dismissed the encounter with Mouse, Turtle, and Antelope. I felt intimately connected with the meadow and the animals, yet I felt isolated and separate in the store, and in many of my everyday experiences. The momentary reverie was disconcerting to my normal sense of myself, and I eagerly embraced that familiar identity as soon as I returned home.

The next day I had another challenging confrontation with my complacency in life. These momentary reveries seemed to just come over me, unbidden. This time it happened while I was waiting at a stoplight while driving to meet my son and his wife for lunch. My car idling behind several other cars, I was absently staring at the red light, anticipating it turning to green. With no warning or transition, I found myself in a grove of redwood trees in Northern California. I was unaware of any animals or people, but I was really tuned in to the giant sequoias. Each one of these massive, powerful trees was a unique personality, and seemingly expressed itself in silent grandeur. *We thrive by joining our root systems, sending water out from the source river to distant brothers and sisters.*

These magnificent beings, each one a striking individual from the ground up, were intricately connected below ground, like a well-engineered irrigation system. The grove I stood in contained about ten trees, and I felt embraced by them. At the same time I felt connected with each one individually, as if each was resonating at a slightly different frequency. And I experienced myself joining with the community, as if I had been initiated into sequoiahood. Above ground I, too, appeared unconnected and separate; yet below ground I felt my rootedness intertwined with the others.

I realized that the light had changed to green when the car behind me gave a short friendly beep. The sequoia grove faded away quickly as I re-entered my everyday world and continued the drive to lunch. But the image of my below ground connection stayed with me vividly.

It was hard to believe that such a profound experience, that seemed so real, could intrude into my life with no preparation and in only a matter of moments. These fragments of experience brought me back to the question I had been asking myself, and had recently forgotten to ask. "Is my experience in this moment a dream, or is this real?" The question was beginning to take on a more imminent significance. And the reveries continued.

One night several days later I was feeling quite spent after a full day of work cutting, splitting and stacking cedar wood for the coming winter's sweat lodges. I was in bed early and, too tired to read, I easily drifted off. It turned out that I worked harder all night long than I had during the day. I was awakened by little people tapping on my bedroom window, demanding that I adjudicate the disputes between them. They impatiently explained that they needed someone outside their species to provide objective judgments, and that they all agreed to abide by my decisions about which party was wronged, and what the compensation should be. Hopelessly awake, I got out of bed and walked to the open window. What I saw outside almost knocked the air from my lungs like a punch to the solar plexus. There were hundreds of gnomes and elves and fairies and leprechauns. They all seemed to be agitated, arguing vehemently with each other, and clamoring for my attention. My heart sank as I realized that there was no refuge for me until I had dealt with every demand.

All night long I listened to grievance after grievance, and made arbitrary judgments. I begged to be left in peace, but that only intensified the din of the crowded meadow outside. It had the same feel to it as the multitudes I dealt with each night of my vision quest years before, except then I got the sense of being in an alternate reality when I occasionally rolled over to get more comfortable physically. This night, standing at the window of my bedroom, there was no rolling over in bed, no interlude of intermission in the dreamlike experience. And this time I asked the question is my experience a dream, or is it real, not as an abstract exercise but as a fundamental reality test. The fact that I could not answer the question sent a shiver down my spine, reminiscent of the first encounter with Owl on my vision quest. This had ceased to be a playful adventure. I was genuinely afraid that I might be going mad. Had I actually fallen down the rabbit hole into an unpredictable and mysterious Under World?

The next morning I awoke on the floor, in front of the open window in my bedroom. I immediately remembered in vivid detail the whole night's work, and I was exhausted. I cancelled several obligations scheduled for the day and went back to bed, falling into a long, deep dreamless sleep.

One more reminder would pierce my complacency in the comfort of a familiar consensus reality. I would soon discover in a shattering blow that 'I' am not separate from 'others', that we are connected to each other and to creation just as surely, if invisibly, as the redwood trees are to each other.[32]

Chapter Eleven
The Guardians at the Threshold

When, through the process and practice of transformation, we no longer experience ourselves as victims of our fate, we can become masters of our destiny.[33]

I went out to the sweat lodge meadow early one afternoon, allowing plenty of extra time before starting the fire for that night's ceremony. I wanted to have some quiet time to ponder the lessons that had been bombarding me faster than I could incorporate them. I cleaned the area of autumn leaves that covered the ground, raking the prairie grass and straightening out the dirt alter. Then I sat in a canvas camping chair next to the stack of cedar wood with my cup of still-warm coffee. The air was clean and brisk, and I sank into a comfortable mental space of no-thought. My senses were full to overflowing with the smells and colors and sounds of my favorite change of season. The presence of animal spirits pervaded the surrounding forest, although I was not aware of any one specifically. I always felt comforted by them.

I heard a voice telling me a story, and I honestly do not know whether I was asleep and dreaming, or daydreaming, or perhaps the source of the voice was just as real as the golden color of the leaves and the squirrel sounds. *This is the ancient story of the hero's journey. But what I most want you to understand is the purpose of the Guardians at the threshold between the hero's community and the Land of the Unknown.* I looked absently at the trees around me, appreciating their beauty and grandeur, and wondering who was the source of this voice. It felt as though the story was being repeated for the thousandth time by the whole living forest/meadow, and I was just fortunate enough to be present for the telling and able to hear it.

The hero always experiences dissatisfaction with life in the conventional world of home, family and culture, and is yearning and searching for something more. This mythic journey always involves a departure from the community and travel to the "otherworld," the Land of the Unknown. At the outskirts of the conventional world, the hero encounters Guardians. They are fierce, dark and dangerous. They are the gatekeepers to insure that only the worthy embark on the journey. They test the strength and resolve of the hero, and in so doing they test his commitment, fortress his strength, and build his stamina. The Guardians prepare the hero for the journey. It seemed to be an incomprehensible riddle: they are a dangerous threat, and they are an empowering ally. The sun and the moon. I reflected on the Guardians preparing me for my journey, the aspects of myself that would limit my development: the fear of becoming lost and of dying, the agitation of a restless mind, the heaviness of torpor and drowsiness that blunts awareness, and the mental laxity in which concentration has no strength. These obstacles were in fact allies, because they forced me to outgrow them, to vanquish them and prevail.

The dragons of darkness may kill and eat the hero, forcing him to resurrect in a new form. Or they may be killed by the hero for him to eat their warrior heart and imbibe their strength. Or the hero may make friends with the dragon, taking him on the journey as a comrade in arms. My addictions had killed and eaten me forty years earlier, and yet I had ultimately found new life, thank God, like Jonah's deliverance from the whale. I was now engaged in overcoming the Guardians of fear and torpor and mental laxity, and strengthening my own capacities in the process. I couldn't help but see as guardians the threatening and demanding emotions exploding out from the liver, those unconscious complexes with a mind of their own. The hero's task is to avoid being overwhelmed by them, and to assimilate them instead.

The living forest/meadow continued storytelling. *The hero's goal is initiation, to find the treasure, the elixir of life, the highest expression of self. Some become seduced upon finding the treasure and succumb to greed; they keep it all for themselves. Most heroes want to bring the treasure back to their community, and undergo additional hardships and challenges in order to do so.*

On returning and approaching the perimeter of the community, the hero encounters new Guardians at the threshold. These, too, are dragons of darkness. Here the hero finds fear of being different, fear of being rejected, the lure of complacency, the self-sabotage of unworthiness. I had known many people over the years who shied away from opportunities to teach or lead or write the book they knew they were capable of, to quit their job and start a business or to tell their spouse how much they loved him/her. They had stopped themselves instead, turned back by the dragons at the threshold. These Guardians, too, offer you their power if you will but take it.

Sitting on my camp chair, basking in the warm wisdom of the forest/meadow despite the autumn chill, I felt a deep sense of contentment. I no longer felt bombarded by my experiences, nor separate from the grass and trees. And curiously, not identified with those emotional explosions that come and go, but also not separate from them. I had a vague sense of my anger and shame and fear as allies, here to help me complete the journey.

Where it came from I cannot say, but to my astonishment another paper message found me, again on two pages, and again at the stack of firewood.

We had to abandon that cave long ago
  Oh, the High Priests hesitated
    And the Council of Elders deliberated
      for long hours
    after the Stranger appeared so suddenly.

He had stood in the narrow opening
      high above
     the cave's dark belly
   that had been the home of our tribe
      to remote ancestors
  and beyond the reach of any legend.

Few could even see him.

He stood without moving for some time
  He seemed to be watching intently for something
      and yet
    He obviously took no notice.

The very old remembered dimly
    the long distant day another man
   had stood high in that same wall - neither could they
     understand now.

Silence fell.

In the hush could be heard his breathing
     rapid   irregular
  the whining gasp of a desperate man.
   And he clutched in his arms
      a box
    of odd dimensions.

He acted the madman
   the High Priests hurriedly consulted
     the Book of Dreams and
      became frightened
  Others saw the panic and it spread

The Stranger suddenly became aware of the horde
                He too seemed frightened and
          making what appeared to be an involuntary wave
                  he dashed back into the rocks
                              out of sight.

Turmoil and chaos
          sacrifices to placate the gods
Terror and violence: nausea.

Those who tried to climb the steep rock wall
                were attacked, beaten and reviled.

Almost to a man those who fled
                the traditional home of our people
          had long before abandoned
                the warmth of that home
                        to live in the far reaches of the cave
                                        apart.

We had nothing to lose by joining the adventure.

All things changed at that narrow opening
                              the primeval apocalypse.
          Having lived as many, we became individuals
                each of us now
                must take step for step himself
along the rough hewn staircase toward each his own destination.

The bottom dropped out
          at that narrow opening
      and freefall surrendered to the pull of
                        an unknown gravity.

Chapter Twelve
The Fieriness of Fire

For a long time I used to think that one should be able to transform suffering into joy. Now, I believe that joy is in discovering that it is OK to suffer. One can be happy at the same time one is suffering! It's OK for there to be a wound. It's part of being human, to have little bits and pieces that are cracked. I play the cello. Some of the eighteenth-century cellos are very badly cracked, but they play more beautifully than the perfectly made modern ones.[34]

Just as at one time, several years earlier, I had successfully incorporated into my daily life the question, "Is this experience a dream, or is it real?" I now noticed consciously, more and more throughout my day, the rising and falling of various emotions. Something would happen and the next thing I knew I was feeling and expressing some activated emotion. Happening to notice the warm sunshine reflecting through the leaves on a nearby Vine Maple tree, a sense of contentment filled my torso, and I unconsciously began to whistle a carefree and happy tune. Only a matter of moments later, my reverie was interrupted by the loud unpleasant honking of a car horn. The feelings in my torso changed immediately to something colder, shallower, more brittle.

The more closely I watched these transient emotions, the more I realized that they were *literally* rising and falling in my body. My attention was drawn to my liver, that dark, impenetrable doorway to the Under World, and the emotions that emerged from it: wrath, jealousy, lust and greed. They seemed to emerge and rise up in the body, growing bigger and more menacing with the ascent through the heart and to the throat. Alternatively, the experience of happiness, intimacy, gratitude and reverence seemed to originate from the heart and throat, and radiate out in all directions. Up to the Upper World, as well as down to the Under World.

One afternoon I sat with a group of angry neighbors who had come together to try to obstruct the county government from approving a code variance requested by an absentee land owner to build a church on our private road. Tempers flared. These people who I knew as friendly and genial seemed to be possessed by explosive rage. I was so fascinated watching the spectacle that I was immune to any contagion of the rage. In fact, although I was sitting in the group, the scene appeared to take place at a distance, as if viewing it through the wrong end of a telescope, and in slow motion. These people, my neighbors, appeared to me more like the little people that came to my window that night, angrily complaining and demanding that I adjudicate their disputes. And I heard a voice speaking to me, the voice of an animal spirit: Hawk. *Give close scrutiny to details which might normally be overlooked.*

With his guidance of what to look for, with careful closer examination, I could observe that the emotions were actually not emerging from the liver. Emerging were vestiges of the unburied dead, lingering at the threshold between the netherworld and my physical reality. I observed some emotions, but they were not wrath, jealousy, lust and greed. What I observed were shame, fear, loneliness, unworthiness, pain, abandonment, and spiritual isolation. These were Guardians standing at the threshold, attempting to repress the Under World and hold these dead marauders from emerging into my reality. A battle of epic proportions unfolded between the intruders and the Guardians.[35]

For one man in the group, the unburied dead was the painful violent humiliation inflicted on him as a seven-year-old child by his gruff grandfather. Somehow the current situation had called out that humiliation lurking just on the other side of the threshold, eager to be energized and given new life.

One of the women looked transparent, and I could see her history captured in time capsule vignettes deep within her body, layer within layer, the earliest embedded deepest. I could see exploding out of a hiding place long denied the raging victim of sexual abuse, perpetrated by a babysitter when she was four. That four-year-old was crazy with vengeance for how she had been violated. Unburied dead was not an apt description for her, because she was not dead but rather the fragment of unlived life still longing to live, of unrevenged betrayal wild to wreak havoc. The life force energy of that four-year-old had split off and retreated into hiding, just as a split-off fragment of the seven-year-old boy had sought refuge from his grandfather. The split-off fragment was the most refined, sensitive, innocent part of the child, and it had to be sent into the *witness protection program* within to preserve it from total destruction, hiding its identity, its very existence. That left another fragment, full of rage and shame, to carry the burden of such a wound: the unburied dead. And so it left a child helplessly dismembered.[36]

The shrillness of Hawk's call pierced my unawareness, encouraging me to look even closer at the slowly developing scene.[37] Within each individual, the unquiet dead were emerging through the portal from the past, usurping existence from the legitimate fragments of unlived life, gone into hiding. The dead charged forward, but had to battle the Guardians that kept them captive. It took immense effort to overcome the loneliness and unworthiness obstacles. They required an infusion of energy from the body, the vital living body of their host, in order to break through. Hawk focused my attention on the channels through which that energy was being activated, usurped.

The emerging fragments struck a chord that resonated with a memory stored in the brain, a languishing ember in the right side of the brain, in the west. And that memory of a distant wounding sparked brightly with renewed energy, as if no time at all had passed since its inception. The memory fanned into flame within the man's brain had the identical feel as when he was seven. The memory that glowed in the woman's brain made her feel just like she did at four. That rejuvenated flare-up within her brain triggered the release of a cocktail of stress hormones sent shooting down into the body, through the intricate system of nerves that connected the brain with the rest of the body, to the heart and lungs with an urgent imperative to fight. The wrath and hatred and fury arose in the deep bowels of the Under World, but only upon instructions from above. And only upon receiving the burst of energy conducted to it, directed by that red nova flare-up in the west, absolutely necessary to wage war with and overcome the Guardians of shame and isolation.

I continued observing the group from this perspective, able to see the layers of wounds within each person there, the archaic fragments roaring their hollow complaints from their confinement in the person's liver, until hitting just the right chord to fan the ember in the brain into flames. Every time that occurred, the unburied dead gained great power over the Guardians, and they escaped into general circulation within the body. How hypnotic and seductive they were, once energized and set loose, marshalling the forces that otherwise would be available for a more productive purpose. And most remarkable was to have all this influence without their presence even being detected, operating on an invisible subterranean level.

Look closely, I heard Hawk say, *and see that emotions are the blood shed by ego*.[38] That blood is the "lifeblood" necessary for existence itself.

Suddenly there was with Hawk another spirit to teach me. Raven encompassed the entire scene, providing the open window through which entered the great mystery of this lesson. Raven was silent, black as midnight, and inscrutable. Yet the truth, reality, seemed to be defined more clearly and simply than ever before. There were no words, just an awareness of the fieriness of fire, the wildness of wind, the turbulence of water, the upheaval of earth, *as well as* the warmth of fire, the coolness and smoothness of water, the gentleness of the breezes, and the goodness, solidity, and dependability of the earth. *You change like the weather, ebb and flow like the tides, wax and wane like the moon.*[39] Raven brought this epiphany from the stillness, the void, where there is nothing yet in form. And back into the void did Raven disappear just as suddenly.

The Guardians at the threshold were just as invisible to their host as the fragments they attempted to imprison, and operated with the same degree of stealth. The Guardians of unworthiness, pain, and abandonment also needed to tap into that same source of energy within the body to do their job. Both sides in this great battle for dominance took sustenance from the same oblivious patron. And when the wildness of wind subsided to the gentleness of calm breeze, that patron continued to provide the needed sustaining support, this time to a different set of influences: satisfaction, quiet reverie, compassion. Yet while the unburied dead were quieted, the part that had gone into hiding in witness protection remained separate, isolated, in cognito. To coax that one out of hiding requires more than just quieting the marauders, but their final and decent burial.

Raven's vision persisted in my mind, with a wondering about the actual process of how these positive emotions become activated and get circulated. And an uncertainty about the useful role that these Guardians might play as allies, as envisioned by the living forest/meadow when it spoke to me.

I found myself sitting with my neighbors again, not distant, not slowed down. They were no longer transparent for me to see the inner workings of the emotional storms coming and going within their bodies. Some of them had calmed down, and were reminiscing warmly about their children now. The battle that had raged only moments ago was quiet, the channels carried only maintenance level activation, and the fieriness of fire had subsided into warmth.

Chapter Thirteen
The Warmth of Fire

The gods have become diseases; Zeus no longer rules Olympus, but rather the solar plexus.[40]

As the neighbors left the meeting place to return home, I felt an odd sense of distance from them, or more accurately an objectivity regarding their emotional state. Several of them were still angry and aggressive toward the people that wanted a zoning variance. Although I could no longer see the fragments battling the Guardians, and the ember in the brain being fanned into flames, I was vividly aware of that process still at work in their bodies. And knowing about the primeval forces involved within this subterranean netherworld, I felt a genuine empathy for each one. What surprised me, however, was the thought that my sense of calm was actually entering and influencing that same netherworld within others. In other words, these emotions were highly contagious. Two things about that thought caught me by surprise: one, that added to the fray within were energies from outside the person, and second, that gratitude and compassion could have a contagious influence just as surely as festering wounds and fear and despair.

Another thought lingered in my mind from the panoramic experience of the evening, and that was the way that Raven had appeared from the void and disappeared back into it. There seemed to be no transition for Raven, no coming and going. He simply materialized, and eventually vanished. I could not hold that possibility. It felt so natural earlier to see the layers of history within people, to know that the forces doing battle had a genesis. The unburied dead had once lived, and the Guardians developed subsequently as a defense. Their history could be traced, and I felt comforted by that knowledge. Yet Raven and the void had no history, they existed outside of history, beyond time. And the truth he spoke was nebulous, not yet fully formed.

In some inexplicable way, the nervous systems of the people that evening had been communicating with each other, silently, unconsciously, like a wi-fi wireless network. I wanted to ponder these things further, to be quiet and unfocused so that the not-yet-fully-formed wisdom could emerge from the void to enlighten me and answer my questions. The evening was cool but inviting, and I selected a huge oak tree standing in a large open space in the public park nearby. I sat down, leaned my back against the solid tree trunk, and became very quiet. Bathed in the cool moonlight, I could hear only my breathing and my heartbeat. I sensed that my breathing was synchronized to my heart's rhythm. I gradually fell into a light, yet very deep, reverie. My heartbeat became more pronounced, dominating my whole experience. It was not just the familiar sound, but the surf-like motion and an indefinable pulsing field of energy. The blood was lapping in and out of a sandy shore, then sent coursing through a narrow inlet, turbulently frothing and foaming. And Dolphin came gracefully swimming up to shore from the deep. Dolphin's breath was exuberant, triumphant. Dolphin, keeper of the sacred breath of life, playfully offered to share the living secrets of access to Dreamtime through the breath, through the heart.

Dolphin's essence is rhythm and pattern, alternating his life first below the surface and then above. My breathing began to follow his rhythm, as I swam below and then above with him. Diving down to explore the depths and returning easily to the surface to breathe once again. Each dive took us deeper, and with each return we lingered longer on the surface. The greater the depth, the darker and more impenetrable was this world. It was indeed the Under World. And yet the blood of life force in which we swam had a primordial intelligence that bridged between the depths and the surface. That intelligence, listened to, regulated our breathing, our heartbeats, and the rhythm of our circulation. Dolphin's freedom of movement conveyed how brain rhythms naturally synchronize to the heart's rhythm. Dolphin exuded love and appreciation, passion and gratitude, and in his circulation upward and downward he coaxed synchrony within the blood pressure and respiratory rhythms, hormone and lymph flow, the organs themselves. Easily moving between the Under World and the Upper World, Dolphin playfully showed me how he weaved harmony throughout his journey.

In the weaving, Dolphin opened to his feminine side, bidden by Grandmother Moon's tidal rhythms. My experience in the cave with Bear

came rushing back to me, how the breath and heartbeat had synchronized, and Bear's meaning in saying that the purpose of entering the cave was to digest past experience and arrive at completion with it. And I had a glimmer of recognition now of what Bear had meant by *womb-cave*. The sea of life force that Dolphin and I were swimming in felt to me very much like Bear's cave, humidly contained and protected, but different in that it was expansive. We dived deeper still, Dolphin teaching me, until we reached the liver, engorged with dark blood. At the opening to the recesses of that organ we could see guardians, but Dolphin was playful with them, good-naturedly teasing them. Dolphin was so comfortable in this Under World, at-home with the darkness, the passions and the turmoil. Waters here were turbulent, the earth in upheaval. Yet Dolphin seemed to be just as at-home up on the surface where the waters were smooth and the earth dependable.

Swimming up to the surface, Dolphin shot out into the humid atmosphere above. He could fly! He seemed to embody Grandfather Sun more as he became more open to Grandmother Moon. What a paradox that seemed to be, that polar opposites could possibly go beyond peaceful coexistence, beyond even complementing each other, to synthesis. Can that apply to the turbulence of water and the smoothness of water? I was also grappling with the dawning awareness that gratitude and compassion could have an influence just as surely as festering wounds and fear and despair. Even more perplexing to me was the vision that energies could be exchanged not only between the Under World and Upper world, between the depths below and the atmosphere above, but also between one person and another, as I had observed within that angry group earlier that evening.

Dolphin swam the answer to this riddle. The heart, the blood circulation system, sent out its message of coherent harmony to all the other systems in the body. Dolphin was the messenger, carrying the word playfully, with exuberance, to every place beneath the surface and beyond. Out into the atmosphere beyond the reach of blood, beyond the skin, out to the space between this body and others.[41] The rhythmic patterns of the heart embody an invitation sent throughout the body *and beyond* to "Come join with me. Come and play." Of course, the same delivery system, the heart's electromagnetic field, can be commandeered by the unburied dead escaped from their confinement in the liver. Then the message of turbulence, fear and despair is carried throughout the body *and beyond.* The contagion of positive or negative emotion is carried from one person to another just like the nutrient water is carried between redwood trees; not through a connected conduit system of roots, but through a wireless conduit system. Our nervous systems are constructed to be captured by the nervous systems of others, so that we can experience others as if from within their skin.[42] *My* feelings can be commandeered by *your* unburied dead! So now I had received another lesson from that night with the little people outside my bedroom window. We are much more closely connected than I ever realized, or dreamed. And as contagious as sadness and anger are, *laughter is the shortest distance between two brains.*

Dolphin's playfulness with the demons in the darkness below showed me a way of reversing the commandeering; I could tame them, keep them from using the body's energy and the heart's delivery system for their own unhealthy purposes. With compassion and gratitude, I could send out the signal inviting harmony. And in doing that, the energy of those demons and their guardians could be commandeered for healthy harmonious purposes. And the energy of someone else's demons run amok, potentially capable of triggering reactions in my body, can also be commandeered for healthy purposes within my body.

Dolphin had more messages for me. Just as emotions spread from mind to mind through that wireless network, so too do ideas. Ideas, beliefs and concepts gather power the same way that the unburied dead do: they associate with strong emotions generated in the depths, in the Under World. Some ideas are naturally incompatible with others, and they go to war. Some ideas are demanding, and they burden their host. Those ideas can fight with each other endlessly, or impose their burden mercilessly, as long as there is emotional energy to draw on from nearby people. These entities that borrow power from strong emotion share a subtle, inexorable magnetism, a gravitylike pull between people that explains the contagion in a group of both laughter and violence.

Another type of entity that borrows power from strong emotion is memories, especially the nagging, recurring ones. Most memories of past events are available to be called upon as needed, but do not intrude unbidden. Traumatic memories, memories attached to deeply emotional hurt, helplessness or regret, also can exert a magnetic gravitylike pull on a person's experience, contaminating their present with an unseen descent into the packed density of what is past. *This dark, implacable entity will invade your mind and body if you allow it, filling you up, leaving little space for pleasure in your aliveness, causing you to squander your present moment.*[43]

The information flow extends not only *beyond the body*, but also *outside time*. Both the heart and brain intuitively respond to information about a future event before the event actually happens.[44] This seemed to explain some of my life experiences, and yet the suggestion of this heart field was becoming more and more incredible.

Dolphin splashed, dived, and literally flew out of the water. The message was clear to me. It is not only people that are connected to this wireless mutual communication system. Animals send out and receive messages on that grid. Trees and flowers and all plant life communicate on the same wireless network. Music can entrain moods and emotions through that network. Spirits and ancestors and angels send and receive using the same field. The earth, the elements, and the directions are connected. The interchange between all aspects of creation is determined by the intensity of emotional energy available to draw on. *Personal separateness is a myth.*

Chapter Fourteen
The Quiet Quest

*God wants to be born in the flame of man's consciousness, leaping
ever higher, and what if this has no roots in the earth - if it is not a
house of stone where the fire of God can dwell but a wretched
straw hut that flares up and vanishes. Could God then be born?
One must be able to suffer God. That is the supreme task for the
carrier of ideas. He must be the advocate of the earth. God will
take care of Himself.*[45]

As I came to awareness of my surroundings, sitting under the tree in
the open field, I felt uplifted by the experience with Dolphin, and
wonderfully calm. I felt as though I was in an eternal moment, and that I
could just stay there for the rest of time. The experience felt full and
complete, yet I also knew that much more awaited my discovery. I felt that
I could discover what existed beyond my current awareness without
leaving this moment, as if I needed only to expand my perception, the
horizon of my awareness, to what was now absent.

Sitting there under the stars, I sensed that Raven had appeared out of
nowhere to shed light on this mystery. *The beyond-the-horizon is an
absence that helps to define the journey, an unseen but vital realm. There
are many invisible absences of what is under-the-ground as well: the other
side of a tree, or of the moon, or of my body, the inside of the tree or moon
or my body. For these would seem to be the two primary dimensions from
whence things enter the open presence of the landscape, and into which
they depart. Sensible phenomena are continually appearing out of, and
continually vanishing into, these two very different realms of concealment
or invisibility. One trajectory is a passage out toward, or inward from, a
vast openness. The other is a descent into, or a sprouting up from, a
packed density.*[46]

I knew that Raven was describing the same truths that Dolphin had,
that diving to the densely packed depths of that ocean of life force could
illuminate and liberate those that had descended there, to sprout up like a
lotus to blossom in the clarity above, and then to enter the vast openness, to
fly through the sky.

The soul, too, is continually appearing out of and vanishing into
concealment, either that of the higher realms and vast openness of the
beyond-the-horizon, or the lower realms and packed density of the *under-*

the-ground. Inexplicably, a Buddhist saying came into my mind, something I had not heard or thought about for many years. *Only to the extent that we expose ourselves over and over to annihilation can that which is indestructible be found in us.*[47] I was confused, because it seemed that annihilation laid in wait in both directions: within the invisible absences *beyond-the-horizon* and *under-the-ground.* What becomes invisible is me. I become invisible, lost into unconscious torpor, in the descent, the low road. And yet I also become invisible, absorbed in transcendence and lost to complacency, in the ascent, the high road. Each alternative, after all, is but a realm to experience and explore. Exposing myself to annihilation while being present for the experience is the great challenge.

Heaven, earth, and human. Beyond the horizon lies a dimension free of condition or form, nothing but vast potential, the void from which Raven had appeared. In the beginning God created the heaven and the earth. And the earth was without form, and void.[48] And God created the Earth and the Seas, the grounding darkness which accommodates everything. Joining the two, the expansive void and the dense ground, heaven and earth, is human, conduit of commerce between them. What is the secret to hovering in balanced suspension between the two? To being *in* the world but not *of* the world? Dolphin's playful navigation between the depths and transcending beyond the confines of the sea itself filled my mind. Heaven above showers us with lifeforce energy, encouraging expansion and outreach. Earth below grounds the lifeforce within us, nurturing digestion and dispersion. Our bodies are built on the same model: the world below, the centers of digestion and elimination, sex and basic physical and emotional needs, are counterbalanced by the world above, the centers of expression, reception, rationality, and the higher needs for aesthetics, self-fulfillment, and selfless service to others.[49] The energy generated below in the fiery furnace of physical survival, manipulation and mastery can be diverted into the great battle for dominance between the marauding unburied dead and the Guardians keeping them captive: the low road. Or it can be elevated to a more peaceful and playful purpose, becoming the ally envisioned by the living forest/meadow: the high road.[50] The energy radiating from above of understanding, intuition and connectedness can be hoarded to feed narcissism and complacency. Or it can be used as fuel for the furnace below to bring the kingdom of heaven within out into the world. *Heaven, earth, and human.*[51]

And the interface, the synthesis, between the two is the heart and the breath, regulated through the world above and the world below, that of intention and that of instinct. The heart is the marriage of matter and spirit, of concrete and abstract, of knowledge and wisdom, of earth and heaven.[52] Now some marriages are blissful, receiving the attention and nurturance necessary to fulfill a mighty potential; some are stormy; some end in suicide or homicide, leaving a mortally wounded survivor to falter and fade.

And now I remembered the brown owl's lesson from the vision quest so long ago: "Be attentive! Stay conscious! When others are cloudy with confusion, I must be transparently clear. When my experience is dreamlike, I must become lucid," whether I am in the higher or the lower realms. There is an I in the place where they meet in marriage, and the key to compassion and personal sacrifice is conscious breath: Bear's breath of completion, the breath synchronized with the heartbeat, the breath of the womb-cave which brings new life in the fullness of time.

I felt encouraged. I was at peace. The star of my soul had shown its light. And in a blissful reverie sitting under the tree in that open field, I caught a glimpse of another parchment, hidden long ago by unknown benefactors for me to encounter at just this moment.

Still prey to interlude unrest, Tzaddi rouses.

Slowly, deliberately
          from her vantage point study
                    bedecked with greens and flowering colors
                    growing among the books and candles
                              and windows
          will Tzaddi sift through her recent experiences.

Calm, restful calm warming her heart,
          content to amble in her search.
There exist some missing fragments
          and I can find them now.

Musing, new memories at her command,
          Tzaddi is more accepting. She listens
                    to her heart more quietly,
                    and understands the freedom of her choice
          to relax the burning impatience
                    that blistered time
                    when she took leave,
                              adventures unremembered and undone.
Now she has the time,
          now
          to reflect in safety
          on her recent narrow escapes
                    from Thanatos.
Twice has she lost control,
                    consciousness,
          to the thief of self-destiny,
                    the frightening titan
                    beguiling and embroiling.

Tzaddi knows her whereabouts here
          for she is at home in her quiet study.
And she knows that through all her
            searches far and near,
      in all the labors and terrors of her quest,
           she need but remember:

         <u>When you have found the beginning
             of the way,
       the star of your soul will show its light</u>.

And not regretfully reflecting
         upon her lapses into time
           for in darkness, germination.

Having fallen into bondage
        and fallen out again,
           the Wheel of Fortune continues on aspin.
Spinning into being
        such involving interludes
        as to rhapsody surrender
                there and then.

And all the while
        absorbing Tzaddi
        embracing
        inviting
        germinating metamorphosis.

And come a dawn ascending
        will spawn
           an altogether sensible
                presence.

Chapter Fifteen
Further Discoveries Within

What Shall I Be
I have again and again grown like grass;
I have experienced seven hundred and seventy moulds.
I died from minerality and became vegetable;
And from vegetativeness I died and became animal.
I died from animality and became man.
Then why fear disappearance through death?
Next time I shall die
Bringing forth wings and feathers like angels:
After that soaring higher than angels –
What you cannot imagine. I shall be that.[53]

The journeys into my body that had been so helpful to me continued. Previously it was to my belly, to my liver, that dark, impenetrable doorway to the Under World. That was my only experience with journeying inside my body, and so I had formed an expectation that any such journey would begin with breaking away from the consensual reality, followed by a long, deep retreat inward, deep into the psyche, and backward in time to prehistory, through a chaotic series of encounters and darkly terrifying experiences. This time I encountered order, experiencing a fulfilling, harmonizing presence that gave me a centering initiation to return to my life with.[54]

This time, instead of going down deep, I found myself entering my head, through the nostrils and into the brain. I knew that I needed guidance, and this time I had the presence of mind to ask for help, even though I really didn't know who I was asking.

I faintly remembered the map that Bear had once communicated to me, with the South in the direction of my forehead, and the North in the direction of the back of my head. The right brain lay in the West, and the left brain in the East. While I felt comforted by having this orientation, I could not fathom the meaning of the information. I clearly needed help.

Know what I know. The thought came floating toward me as if carried on the rays of friendly morning light. *Follow the natural progression of my journey, and you will understand.* Butterfly humbly offered me her story. It unfolded in images, vignettes of transformation from egg to larva to cocoon and finally to the birth of the butterfly.[55] First there is a beginning, an egg stage, that primordial yet delicate emerging from the pregnant potential of the unseen and unspoken, not yet altogether a reality in this world. Butterfly reminded me of how Raven, too, emerged from the stillness, the void, where there is nothing yet in form. In due time the egg stage grows into the larva, allowing for development from conceptus to being. Here is provided initiation, introduction to the new world, an inkling of what could be, of what is to come. Here strength of character is nurtured and 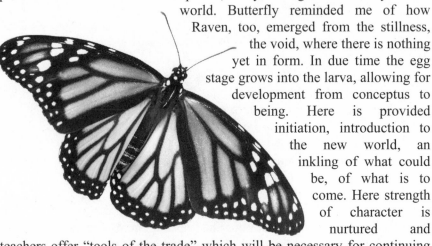 teachers offer "tools of the trade" which will be necessary for continuing the journey. The larva stage gives way to the cocoon stage, where one goes within, sheltered in the swaddling clothes of timeless repose. Bear enters the cave, the *womb-cave*, to digest past experience and arrive at completion with it. And in the fullness of time comes birth for the butterfly, fully-formed and prepared to fulfill its purpose.

I felt calmed by the tranquil presence of Butterfly. There was no hurry to move from one stage to the next, and yet each new stage of transformation incorporated what had come before. And so each new stage expanded what had come before, at once leaving it behind, completed and to be buried, and yet bringing it into this timeframe, incorporated, elaborated, liberated.

Despite feeling so calm and unhurried, I felt some frustration at not understanding the relevance of Butterfly's story to my view at the threshold of the brain. I wanted to comprehend, but it seemed so much more complex here than the primitive scene of the liver, the unburied dead and the guardians. I had many questions, especially what guardians served here at the threshold of each new stage?

Chapter Sixteen
The Lesson of the Luggage

Tanzan and Ekido were once traveling together down a muddy road. A heavy rain was still falling. Coming around a bend, they met a lovely girl in a silk kimono and sash, unable to cross the intersection.

"Come on, girl" said Tanzan at once. Lifting her in his arms, he carried her over the mud.

Ekido did not speak again until that night when they reached a lodging temple. Then he no longer could restrain himself. "We monks do not go near females," he told Tanzan, "especially not young and lovely ones. It is dangerous. Why did you do that?"

"I left the girl there," said Tanzan. "Are you still carrying her?"[56]

Still sitting in reverie under the tree in that open field, I felt as if time was standing still. Images flashed before me of some of my recent adventures, of Raven and Dolphin, of Sun and Moon. I felt warm, and satisfied. An image came upon me, dimly outlined yet vividly detailed, of the vision quest with Owl. I easily entered into the fourth night's dreams in which I was on the security staff at an airport, watching people file past with their luggage, on the way to boarding a plane. They all seemed uncertain and confused. And then a realization hit me with the impact of a falling brick: there was a profound connection between their confusion and their luggage! Preoccupation with the baggage seemed to eclipse their ability to attend to their immediate experience. How different it might be for each of these people if they were free of the burden of packing and repacking it, carrying it, watching and guarding it, keeping track of it. *Wherever you go, there you are. Your luggage is another story.*[57]

What luggage was I carrying that slowed me down or kept me preoccupied? The probing question seemed to demand exploration, yet I continued to feel calm and unhurried. Certainly I could see how possessions often fit that description. And I could see how certain burdensome memories might as well. Then a remarkable sight came into view, in the center of the brain: a "smoke detector" to alert us when the heat of negative emotion becomes hazardous.[58] That smoke detector operates instinctually. It bypasses thinking and speaking altogether. It is vigilant for the comings and goings of intense negative emotion, alert to what lies beyond-the-horizon, to what is under-the-ground, or to what *might be*, and especially to what *was*. This smoke detector goes off even when it is *reminded* of a once threatening fire, or when it *anticipates* the possibility of smoldering embers to come. Such is the nature of luggage. Preoccupation with the baggage can eclipse our ability to attend to our immediate experience.

Have you ever tried to think clearly, or communicate coherently, with a smoke detector blasting away in your ear, shattering any hope of concentration, let alone tranquility? What a huge challenge that presents. Yet even greater is the difficulty of allowing the heat and fire to flare up without leaving a trace of smoke to set off the alarm. Is it possible to separate fire from smoke? Raven's lesson came to mind: we cannot separate the fieriness of fire from the warmth of fire. But fieriness is fire's essential nature; smoke is its baggage. I was getting confused, and needed guidance. I felt like reaching out to unknown resources, asking for help in understanding this confusing maze.

Recognizing their absolute nature makes it possible to free thoughts as they emerge at the source, in such a way that they leave no traces.[59] Fire is fiery, and it is warm. It only produces smoke when it is left to smolder. Manage to embrace the essence of every experience, without becoming preoccupied, without baggage, without a trace.

Once again I became aware of sitting under the tree in that open field, accompanied by Raven and Dolphin, Sun and Moon, Bear and Butterfly. My mind was quiet, my soul was still. The tide was in.

Chapter Seventeen
Profound Groundedness

The call of the whale is the lullaby of the tides.[60]

Over the following weeks I gratefully returned to the groundedness of everyday chores. Relishing my morning coffee and paying the bills seemed just as profound, and as reassuring, as Sun and Moon. My wife and I decided to take a vacation to Mexico, to lay on the beach, fish for marlin, and snorkel.

On our third day there we traveled to a remote beach on the Sea of Cortez to snorkel on the protected coral reef. Underwater is such a different world, where the fish are at home and a sense of timelessness reigns. A group of curious sea lions swam under us, as graceful in that environment as any ballet dancer could be in hers. Their unblinking eyes were riveted on us, sad and playful, without judgment. And then we climbed back into our small outboard boat to return to our origins on the beach, back to where we are at home, if not timeless. On the way, our young guide spotted a humpback whale breaching the water magnificently, and he headed the boat directly for it. Approaching the whale, we realized there were two: a mother and her baby. The mother only surfaced every ten minutes or so, while the calf came up for air every two or three minutes. These creatures were at once more alien than any animal I had ever seen and more familiar than my own heritage.

During the intervals between surfacings, my wife and our guide were talking excitedly about "la Ballena grande" and laughing with glee. My awareness began to sink deeper underwater, down to a shadowy and dreamlike world. Whale's realm felt like a vast library, repository to ancient and arcane knowledge. I had the sense of wanting to be silent, respectful of the accumulated wisdom of all the earth's generations. Somehow these regal scholars were caretaking the archives of earth's history. Whale had integrated the knowledge and carried it incorporated into her bodily organism. Whale *embodied* the wisdom of the ages.

Wisdom requires consistently consolidating all that you know, and pruning it by unlearning what you cannot enact in ceremony and carry in your body. Use your Dreamtime for reverse learning.[61] Was Whale using metaphor to teach me? Surely she could not mean what she said literally. It seemed ultimately reasonable in that dreamy underwater realm. But what did it mean in my world? *Develop your capacity for disattention as well as attention.* I began to feel almost flooded with a subtle understanding of the apparent paradox. This capacity plays a central role in the shaman's visionary experience, in a hypnotized person's focus on an internally generated environment, and the quiescent periods of meditation.[62] It is the same capacity as becoming deeply engrossed in imaginative activities producing vivid imagery, reverie and daydreams, and engaging in holistic thinking. Call it "mild mystical experience" or "flow": a joyous and creative total involvement with life.[63] These abilities are also characteristic of dreams.[64]

I had the same experience of intimacy that I did with Bear in his cave, the *womb-cave*, except there it felt tightly contained and here in Whale's world I felt expansive, as if the entire environment was wide open unlimited horizon. Bear had shown me the purpose of entering the cave, to digest past experience and arrive at completion with it. Whale was now showing me what to do after reaching completion: let go of the past, open to visions of the horizon, dream.

With the smoke detector quiet, allow the GPS in the brain to rest also. The GPS? This underwater realm did seem to soften negative emotions: no smoldering fires to produce smoke, no blaring smoke detector. Although I had never thought of it as a GPS, I did have a faint recollection of an area of the brain in the upper rear known as the orientation association area. This was located within the direction of Dreamtime in the North, Whale's realm. This is where we get our ability to orient ourselves in space and time, which gives our bodies a sense of physical limits. It is also where the brain "makes" our sense of an individual "self" existing apart from the rest of the physical universe. This part of the brain goes dark when one dives inside, when the outside world recedes, effectively blocking the sensory input that ordinarily streams into our brains. With no information flowing into that area, the brain cannot create a boundary between self and outside world, or locate itself in physical reality. As a result, it has no choice but to perceive that self as endless, interwoven with everyone and everything.[65]

Whale offered the recipe for creating the myriad forms of mystical experiences known to seekers across time and culture: the shaman's visionary experience; quiescent periods of meditation; the euphoric, otherworldly states described by Christian mystics and Jewish Kabbalists, Himalayan yogis and Sufi whirling dervishes, Buddhist meditators and whales. Quiet the smoke detector and the GPS in the brain. But how?

Consolidate all that you know, and prune it. Develop your capacity for disattention as well as attention. It seemed impossibly paradoxical. How was I to do this? I sensed instinctively that it must be related in some way to the tides, the lullaby of the tides. But how?

There are many rest-activity cycles throughout our lives. Every day we digest and sleep, everyday we eat, work, and play. This cycle is active during sleep, too, creating the cycles of rapid eye movement (REM, dreaming) and non-rapid eye movement (NREM, nondreaming). This is the 2- to 3-hour ultradian rhythm of alternating brain activity between the right hemisphere and the left. It influences every aspect of life, from mood and emotion to intelligence and mental performance. REM sleep, and activation during waking, correspond with greater activity in the left hemisphere, higher blood pressure, and fight-or-flight stress response. NREM sleep, and waking non-activity, correspond to greater activity in the right hemisphere, lower blood pressure, and the freeze stress response.

One function of dream (REM) sleep is to find and remove undesirable modes of mental processing in the brain. Such modes are detected and suppressed by a special mechanism that operates during REM sleep and has the character of an active process that is the opposite of learning. *Use your Dreamtime for reverse learning.* Whale seemed to almost blush with embarrassed self-consciousness when she added, *whales and dolphins have mastered the process of unlearning, so our sleep is uninterrupted – unihemispheric.*[66] *But I can teach you how to master it too.*

My head was almost reeling with all the information. I wanted to give up, to rouse myself from the connection with Whale, and rest. I felt the need to stop the flow of stimulation, find a place of quiet, and take the time to assimilate what I had absorbed. And I knew that I could, yet I was drawn as if to a magnet by the prospect of learning the secret to mastering consolidating and pruning, attention and disattention.

The organizing wind of the Breath of Life arises from the Dynamic Stillness, producing rhythms within rhythms.[67] Some of the body's rhythms are much more brief than 2 or 3 hours. There is a long tide, a deep and slow rhythmic impulse of about 1½ to 2 minutes in duration that emerges from a deep ground of stillness at the center of our being. A mid-tide is about 25 seconds long, and another rhythm is about every 5 seconds.

First, know that there is a little gap in the transitional moments between rest and activity in any of these cycles, whether during sleep or awake time. That momentary interlude that is neither one nor the other is a sublime pure consciousness, a silent void, the deep ground of stillness at the center of our being.[68] Whale was conveying something very profound to me about an opening into an entirely new way of being. Yet it is an experience that all of us have every day, unknowingly. Whales and dolphins can live in that way of being, neither on one side nor the other but hovering in between. An exhilarating thrill shot through me as I realized Whale was about to teach me how to hover there too.

Integrate the chaotic sea of rhythmic changes with your breath. Pay attention and you will discover that, awake or asleep, during times of left hemisphere dominance (active phase, REM sleep), the airflow in your natural breathing is greater through your right nostril. Likewise, during right hemisphere dominance (resting phase, NREM sleep), the airflow is greater through your left nostril. Deliberately breathing through the right nostril stimulates the active phase and deliberately breathing through the left nostril stimulates the resting phase. When the smoke alarm is blaring, provide an antidote by breathing through the left nostril, which lowers heart rate, blood pressure, and fight-or-flight (stress) activity. When you want to stimulate your energy level, breathe through the right nostril. Alternating between left and right nostril breathing harmonizes the body's physiological and psychological systems.[69] *Bring to consciousness the state you create.*

Whale was teaching me how to integrate dream consciousness within waking consciousness. And, possibly, waking consciousness within dream consciousness, too.

I gradually became aware of the excited laughter and awe that the two others with me in our small boat were expressing. I shared their exuberance, and yet I felt very much still in a dream. Just at that moment both mother and baby breached the surface two boat lengths from us. Their tails splashed cool salt water on us, and I began to rouse more completely from my reverie. We knew they were diving deep and swimming fast for open ocean, surrendering to the unlimited horizon they could both see ahead.

Chapter Eighteen
Embodying the Wisdom of the Ages

Short Cuts
There are indeed short cuts to higher knowledge.

Those to whom the idea of a short cut appeals are the least likely to be able to use them.

This is because these tend to be the people in whom the factor of greed is so strong that it screens off the capacity to benefit from the short cut.

A straight line is not the shortest journey between two points if the distant point is so screened that you may see it but not reach it.

A man who arrives at the door of a house before anyone else may feel self-satisfied, not knowing that he has forgotten to bring the key.[70]

The remainder of our vacation was heavenly. My wife in her feminine wisdom balanced lazy days on the beach with activities in the nearby Mexican village. Sun and Moon, sunbathing and fishing, a natural ultradian rhythm. And then we were ready to return home to our everyday schedules.

Once home, I experienced a strange consequence of the encounter with Whale. I felt like I had now found the quiet place to rest from the rigor of absorbing so much information that I really did not understand. I didn't think about it, in fact I tried to keep it at bay. However, from time to time during the day, every day, it dawned on me that I was aware of the rhythm of my body. I was unintentionally becoming more in tune with that feminine wisdom within. And the ultradian rhythm created lows in which the dream mode of consciousness was penetrating into the waking mode.[71] Living in unison with the dream, I could stop chasing it. Even if only from time to time, now and then.

If my days were more calm and quiet, my sleep seemed to be more active. Dreams were vivid, dramatic, wild. Some part of my awareness remained awake even while the rest of my brain slept. Dreamless sleep became a profoundly nourishing dip into the great deep.

Looking back, I can see that this was a period of consolidation and integration. At the time, I was amiably uninformed about what was happening to me. Yet I also was beginning to realize that I could take charge of my experience, that changes in my actual state of being were possible, and could be made voluntarily, intentionally. That realization was no more blindingly presented than when I stumbled across another parchment, this one folded roughly and stuffed into the pages of an old used book I picked up in my favorite book shop. It stopped me in my tracks, and yet was somehow reassuring at the same time.

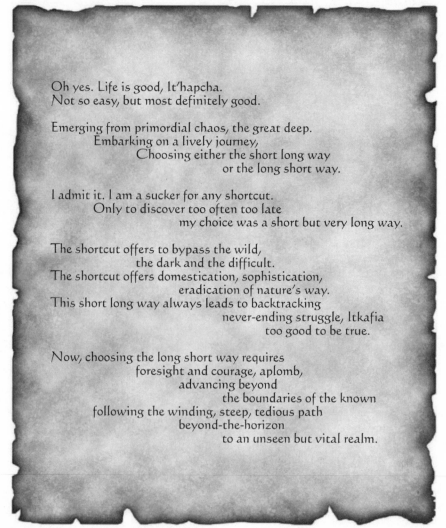

Oh yes. Life is good, It'hapcha.
Not so easy, but most definitely good.

Emerging from primordial chaos, the great deep.
    Embarking on a lively journey,
        Choosing either the short long way
            or the long short way.

I admit it. I am a sucker for any shortcut.
    Only to discover too often too late
        my choice was a short but very long way.

The shortcut offers to bypass the wild,
        the dark and the difficult.
The shortcut offers domestication, sophistication,
        eradication of nature's way.
This short long way always leads to backtracking
          never-ending struggle, Itkafia
            too good to be true.

Now, choosing the long short way requires
        foresight and courage, aplomb,
          advancing beyond
            the boundaries of the known
following the winding, steep, tedious path
        beyond-the-horizon
          to an unseen but vital realm.

Transforming darkness into light
requires taking the long short way
through the wild, the dark and the difficult.
Rising and falling like the tides
and rising again not in conquest over
a vanquished foe,
but rising in triumphant holy service
lifting profane into sacred,
banal into extraordinary.

The long but very short way follows a soulful rhythm,
the crashing of the tides
with its ups and downs
leading steadily, stealthily
to the precarious certainty of
indwelling mastery.

The soul has reached its precarious perch between
giving in to the consuming desire to go home,
to pour itself into the embrace of the Father,
and
giving in to the seduction of nourishment,
to stay home,
to fit itself into the containment of the Mother.

Bring into this body the long but short way home.

Chapter Nineteen
Judgment

What we oppose, we confirm.
What we avoid, we oppose.
What we grasp, we violate.
What we cling to, clings to us.
What we destroy, destroys us.[72]

The days were becoming longer, trees greening with new leaves, and I was feeling a contented expectancy with the springtime.

Quietly sitting on the porch one morning, listening to the birds sing and the trees rustle in the breeze, I suddenly burst out laughing, recalling the night some years before when I had been awakened by wee people tapping on my bedroom window, demanding that I adjudicate the disputes between them. I was amused at how startled I had been by the horde of gnomes and elves and fairies and leprechauns. And, like so many of my experiences, I really didn't know how real it was. But I did know, sitting on my porch, that it was immensely comical, although even now somewhat unsettling.

It began to dawn on me that there was an aspect of sanctuary in the experience of those little people, an interlude of refuge, of protection from predators (each other). It seemed contradictory that anyone would feel asylum while being judged. *Bringing rationality together with emotionality brings relief by turning off the blaring smoke detector.* Children feel secure when they have clear boundaries, and enforcement of established consequences for violations. We all do, much as some of us hate to admit it. Connect the left brain's cause-effect reasoning with the right brain's intense emotion and holistic big-picture thinking. Bring both hemispheres fully online for peace of mind.

Vaguely aware of sitting on the porch that morning, I was much more aware of a presence nearby that felt safe, even protective. That presence seemed to know The Law, and to apply the knowledge of it with balance. *I am Crow, the Left-Handed Guardian. I know the unknowable mysteries and I am the keeper of all sacred law. I live in the Void, and I merge light and darkness.*[73] Crow had whispered the thought about bringing rationality together with emotionality, and now I was beginning, barely, to comprehend the depth of the lesson to be learned from Crow. This information was related in some way to sanctuary, and to judgment, and to what more I could not even guess.

Understand that I am a shadow, and I come to you from the Void. She pacified my fears through telling me her history. *Long ago I was fascinated with my own shadow. I kept looking at it, scratching it, pecking at it until my shadow woke up and came to life. Then my shadow ate me, and I became Dead Crow.* She was prepared to share all that she knew, yet she was warning me that much of that knowledge was inaccessible to me, unknowable. I felt honored by Crow's presence. That history helped me to glimpse the meaning of her statement about merging light and darkness, for she is shadow, she is both Crow and Dead Crow. I experienced nothing sinister or intimidating about her, yet I was immanently aware of Crow's profound power, the authority bestowed on the keeper of sacred law.

One thing about Crow's message was clear: if we put our energy into our shadow side, it becomes strengthened and eventually it will split off from the whole self and devour us. Energizing the shadow can come from indulging it, or denying and thwarting it, or channeling expression of the shadow into rage, fear, aggression, and arousal. I could see a montage of numerous moments from my life in which I had become possessed by a part of myself intent on sabotaging my highest good.[74] These moments are times when the undead souls escape their confinement in the liver, wreaking their havoc, triggering the alarm of the smoke detector.[75]

I was grateful to Crow for sharing her personal history, because it helped me to understand a little better the relevance of her comments about bringing rationality together with emotionality, and merging light and darkness. What is the connection to sanctuary and to judgment? *You must expand your point of view, far beyond this earth and the human law that governs it.* My mind began racing to understand. *Human law is not the same as Sacred Law. If you obey the Sacred Law, then at death you die a Good Medicine death.* I felt so limited in my ability to understand. I wanted to expand my point of view, but talking about Sacred Law and death was incredibly challenging. *A Good Medicine death allows you to benefit from the review that is provided, which you call Judgment.* I was beginning to grasp her meaning. It was slowly coming into focus for me, as if the message was emerging out of a foggy background. The little people outside my window on that night so long ago had sought out my judgment, accepted it unquestioningly, and quieted their raucous emotional chaos. They needed perspective and discernment – rationality – to augment what was not available within. Surely Crow was telling me that this is identical to what my experience will be when I die.

The judgment that will be provided for me following this life will reflect a perspective and discernment far beyond my own by a great Master who sees simultaneously the three fates: past, present, and future. The Master will assist me in a life review. If I die with rage in my heart, or fear, or aggression, or greed, I probably won't fully embrace the feedback I receive as helpful. The more defensive I am, the more preoccupied with myopic self-indulgances, the less I will benefit. If I die with one of those complexes in charge, hijacked and possessed by a shadow, that shadow will eat me and I will not die a Good Medicine death. I was beginning to feel a growing respect for the little people who had come to me that night, because they had sought judgment, had accepted it openly, and had found sanctuary in it.

Crow interrupted my wandering thoughts. *One more thing. You wanted to know how ultradian rhythm is related. Sacred Law provides many opportunities every day to experience a Good Medicine death. Every ebb and flow of the tides is an ending and a new beginning.* If I allow one moment to expire with rage in my heart, or fear, or greed, then the new beginning to follow will be limited instead of advanced through the benefit of review, judgment, acceptance and sanctuary.

The Void that I speak of, where I live, where infinite light and endless darkness merge and earthly opposites unite, creates sanctuary for humans to step outside time, outside who they think they are, into a pure pleasure of being. Such is Good Medicine death: a breathtaking sunset or defenseless intimacy, experienced from the void.

Chapter Twenty
Rhythm of the Dark

Achaan Chaa looked down and smiled faintly. He picked up the glass of drinking water to his left. Holding it up to us, he spoke in the chirpy Lao dialect that was his native tongue: "You see this goblet? For me, this glass is already broken. I enjoy it; I drink out of it. It holds my water admirably, sometimes even reflecting the sun in beautiful patterns. If I should tap it, it has a lovely ring to it. But when I put this glass on a shelf and the wind knocks it over or my elbow brushes it off the table and it falls to the ground and shatters, I say, 'Of course.' But when I understand that this glass is already broken, every moment with it is precious."[76]

Springtime continued to unfold. And so did my understanding of ultradian rhythms and Good Medicine death, or at least I thought that is what my growing understanding was about. I really didn't know how the information came to me. But I was confident that trustworthy and knowledgeable elders were willing to teach me, and they knew how to establish contact. The most important aspect of this was that they knew how to establish contact, whereas I didn't know how and couldn't initiate the interactions. In fact I was always surprised when it happened.

I puzzled over the enigma of being contacted like this, being offered mind treasures, hidden *terma*, by the wise ones. And part of my bafflement was that these wise ones were not human, wizened old wizards or crones, but rather animals! Crow and Whale, Bear and Mountain Elk, it suddenly seemed fantastic, unreal. And yet during the experience with each of them I was as coherent and rational as I am capable of being. Until that point in time I had not questioned the reality of these experiences, I had simply accepted them. But I was exceedingly curious about the how and the why.

I knew that further exploration of my brain was necessary, and first I launched into researching everything I could find to read about the things that Crow had told me. That proved to be frustrating, and not very fruitful. One day I sat staring at a multicolored drawing of the brain from a neuroscience textbook, fascinated to the point of becoming spellbound. Each of the different parts of the brain were brightly colored and labeled with their exotic names – Thalamus, Parietal lobe, Corpus callosum, Superior colliculus. The more I stared at the drawing, the more beautiful it became and the more entranced I became. Gradually the labels on the page blurred, the irregular shapes began to vibrate with energy, and I was transported into a very different world.

I became aware of a drive for wakeful consciousness in the ultradian pacemaker, and a sleep gate there that opens when consciousness fades and closes when wakefulness reasserts itself.[77] And then I became aware of an area that could turn itself off to create a sense of empty headedness, no-thought.[78]

I became aware of an energy membrane separating me from other levels of reality; that's the only way I can describe it. I was in the center of the brain, in the center of the Medicine Wheel. There was a small structure there whose activity increases in darkness and decreases in the light. Emanating from this place were the visionary activities of dreams and mystical states. It distorts space and time perception, awareness of being a human ego/self, and has the uncanny tendency to open the door of emergence into an alien world.[79] It is not the GPS that I had already encountered, but rather an interdimensional GPS. Just as the unburied dead inhabit the liver, so 'other beings' inhabit realms that exist on the other side of that door. I knew instinctively that this membrane was all that separated me from Crow and Whale, Sun and Moon, ancestors and elders. Having found the door, could I initiate contact with them?

Aware again of staring at the brightly colored drawing, I felt separate from it, and yet oddly connected to the living organ I had just visited. I experienced a sudden thunderstorm of recognition, recalling the day so long ago that I had first encountered Bear who was raiding my birdfeeder. Overtaken with drowsiness, I had collapsed onto the ground and fallen asleep in a state of nonbeing, to be visited by cockroaches communicating telepathically and giant sequoia trees, and a circle of people that I "knew" without knowing anything of their life circumstances or histories. Now I was learning about the doorway through which I had entered those other dimensions, or rather through which they had entered into mine. The sleep gate had opened, and in the darkness that door had opened too.[80] It was too vast for me to comprehend, imponderable yet undeniable.

Chapter Twenty-one
The Trickster's Crazy Wisdom

There is nothing so whole as a broken heart.[81]

More often now I experienced that sudden burst of laughter, as I had recalling the night of the wee people. Things that happened seemed to just strike my funny bone in unpredictable ways.

An example is an experience that occurred following an extended period of meditation with a particular spiritual teacher, Shree Maa. I had spent many years in personal therapy dealing with my resentment toward my parents for "borrowing" money from me in my teenage years, and never repaying it. I felt used, and forced into a position of age-inappropriate responsibility. A behavior pattern that developed from that early experience was hyper self-reliance. The day after the meditation retreat with Shree Maa, I happened to go searching in a box in my office closet for some professional documents I needed regarding renewal of licensure. I had periodically accessed such important papers in that box over the previous twenty years. On this occasion, I discovered at the top of the pile of papers in the box, never having encountered it previously, a cancelled check written by my parents to me forty years earlier, repaying the money borrowed. My fourteen-year-old endorsement was carefully written on the back of the check. The moment brought my ego, invested for so long in its version of personal history, close to the edge of disintegration. Immediately I experienced a moment of ecstatic humor and liberating clarity. Finding that cancelled check was the funniest, most ironic, and most humbling experience of my life. I couldn't stop laughing, and the moment seemed to last a lifetime. That moment offered an opportunity for a great opening to occur, vast and spacious, novel and spontaneous.

For days following that epiphany, I had many surprising capricious moments. I spilled a pitcher of cream when I retrieved it from the refrigerator, and immediately recognized the jagged effects of too much coffee. I laughed at myself. Later that day, I was driving through town and saw ahead of me an attractive young woman walking along the sidewalk. As I drove past, I glanced over to see her face and realized "she" was a bearded man with flowing long hair. The absurdity of my assumptions seemed hilarious.

I was enjoying these little surprises as they popped up in my life, and a general sense of lightness was lifting my spirits in a new way. I was coming to expect the humorous each day, and with it came a sense of innocence and wonder. Then one morning while I was pondering these things, a thought came to me. These experiences were not random – they were being provided to me for my benefit, my growth. But these serendipitous moments were orchestrated by an invisible hand, unlike so many of the lessons I had been given, or so I believed. Of course, I immediately realized that finding the cancelled check was a lesson offered by my spiritual teacher Shree Maa. That I found it the day after the meditation retreat was no coincidence. But what about these other instances of seemingly cosmic humor? Where did the magic and the serendipity come from? Or were they only whimsy?

I recognized my own foolishness. And that, it turns out, serves an important spiritual purpose. It forced me to go beneath the surface of experience, to question all the things I took for granted in my everyday life, and to explore the outer reaches of conventional beliefs. *Seize the present moment in all its freshness.*[82] Call it crazy wisdom. The Native American tradition holds that Coyote, the Joker, the great Trickster, carries this way of whimsical reflection. But Coyote tends to be fooled by his own trickery, and no one is more astonished than Coyote at the outcome of his own tricks.[83] The invisible hand orchestrating these surprises was more wise than fool, yet willing to use a magical, fun, even crazy method of delivery. I laughed at the thought of this crazy Coyote; I felt inspired to call him the Fool Coyote.

Crazy wisdom goes beyond all reference points. Relax into insecurity and the absence of any stable ground. Learn to navigate in the abyss, the chasm without bottom. It is okay, even though there is no hope of understanding anything at all. Give up your ambition to put the jigsaw puzzle together. Give it up altogether, absolutely; throw it up in the air, put it in the fireplace. Unless we give up this hope, this precious hope, there is no way out at all.[84] The Fool Coyote spoke his foolishness, and showed me mine through a more accurate reflection of reality than any mirror could ever provide.

I realized that I would need to allow the true meaning of Fool Coyote's messages to sneak up on me. He was speaking to me about living spontaneously, experimentally, in close contact with my instinctual side, my animal nature. *Live carefree, embody the gusto that enlivens, dance with the life-principle. Be honest enough to acknowledge the ways you have conned yourself, and celebrate the genius of your self-deception.*

I had to laugh with recognition. How often was I the emperor with no clothes, the only one foolish enough to believe my own fabrications? How often do I take myself so seriously that I cannot see the obvious? How often do I still not believe it, even when the obvious is made painfully undeniable?

There was a sense of sadness here, too, exquisite sadness, sadness uncontaminated by guilt or regret. Fool Coyote was calling me to account, as well as calling me to live my life with passion. To do so is to live with my heart open and vulnerable, courageously defenseless.[85] And how could a person live in such a way without sadness for the world? *When you stay in tune with your own heart and feel its quality without judging it or impulsively reacting to it, you will discover beneath all the emotional highlights a deeper, tender, more constant feeling. At the core of the heart is a sense of profound, unwavering sadness and joy that comes from being truly open to the world and responding deeply to it.*[86] Sadness and joy are each the experience of the heart full to overflowing.

Raven appeared out of nowhere to bring me the gift of paradox. *The most ancient name for the Heart, anahata, means "the sound that is created without any two things striking," or "the sound that is produced by no cause, that originates from the Void."*[87] Crow, keeper of all sacred law, lives in that Void, merging light and darkness, creating sanctuary. Only by fully accepting the miraculous conception of our deepest core can it be experienced as full to overflowing. Only to the extent that we expose ourselves over and over to annihilation can that which is indestructible be found in us.

Chapter Twenty-two
The Sun

Consciousness evolves when the self dissolves.[88]

At the core of the heart is a sense of profound, unwavering sadness and joy. Over a period of several weeks I had the pleasure of tending fire for three sweat lodges on successive Sunday evenings. Each of those afternoons, sitting by the fire in the open meadow, I pondered sadness and joy. The vivid image of the lotus flower came back to me as it had when I experienced being with Bear in the Dream Lodge so long ago. Again I could sense the stark contrast between the dark, primordial mud from which its roots grow up through the swampy waters and the breathtakingly beautiful blossom floating gently on the rippling surface. Sadness and joy. These, too, are the energies of the moon and the sun. The one is cool, dark, feminine, fertile. The other is the radiant red hot of action, vibration, and the masculine.

I remembered, too, the insights that emerged for me at that time about the fickleness of so many of my emotions, nothing more than the changing weather of the mind, the sudden rain storm or brilliant rainbow. And raising the possibility of finding the perspective of the weatherman who sees and reports on the changing weather without actually being affected by it. It did seem that I was discovering beneath all the emotional highlights a deeper, more constant feeling, the feeling I would call peace of mind.[89]

These afternoons were carefree, timeless, fulfilling. They provided me a glimpse of living in the abyss, with gusto. The meaning of the abyss began to come into focus. How else could you describe living in between sadness and joy, sun and moon, masculine and feminine. Not halfway in between, averaging the two extremes, but suspended one moment at a time in the in-between.

One evening I experienced what I can only describe as ego unintegration following a particularly profound spiritual experience in the sweat lodge. Emerging into the cool evening air, I found myself having no unbidden thoughts in my mind for the remainder of the evening, which entailed a leisurely dinner and conversation with the group. There was no "mind chatter," no sequence of thoughts. Time seemed to have slowed down, and the words or actions in each moment felt curiously like a choice, and yet every interaction seemed to be absolutely spontaneous, without planning or consideration of consequences. It was as if between each action (word, emotional response, laugh, taste) there was pregnant empty space, and in that space lay choice. I embraced the emptiness of that gap, blissfully free from and unburdened by any idea, reference, or concept. "Normal" consciousness returned when I awoke from deep sleep the following morning. The extended experience was the unburdened, wide-open state of Sabbath for personality, taking time off from self, time simply to be.

I am the Law symbolized by Strength, free and fleet as the Wind. A magnificent white stallion stood before me, offering liberation from the limitations of the four kingdoms – nature, mineral, vegetable, and animal/human. *Elevate everything you encounter within the four kingdoms, and you open the door to the Fifth Kingdom.* I did not understand what Horse was talking about. *The lotus, mired in the mud, holds the potential to elevate by growing into the beautiful flower basking in the sunlight.* All things contain within their present form the promise of something greater. As a principle it seemed so simple and obvious. But what role did I play in elevating anything other than myself? *Planting seeds or eating food elevates each, as long as you do so consciously. And only by living consciously are you elevated to your greater potential, to the Fifth Kingdom.*

The image of a burning candle emerged in the air next to Horse. The candle was bright, and cast a warm glow. Then when a glass lamp was placed around the candle, the light it radiated became much brighter. My role of elevating is to both contain and magnify. Creating sacred space safeguards what has been entrusted to my care, and amplifies its value, in the process magnifying mine.[90]

A clear understanding emerged about the deeper meaning of that vision quest with Owl so long ago, and my relationship with all the people who seemed to need me in order to progress. What I was too confused to provide, and really the only thing they needed from me, was my conscious awareness. That would have elevated them. And in order to elevate them, I had to be elevated, mindful, conscious.

Horse unexpectedly presented me with a parchment, and disappeared, leaving behind for me the warm radiant glow of the candle lamp.

"Resurrection! That's what I want."
        Well, when the youngster demanded this
                I was certainly surprised -
          not so much at the request
              for it was often chosen;
      but that such a young boy should ask it.

He couldn't have been more than seven
              or ten at most
        and like all children
      he may have been afraid
        of the lion that chased him
              up the monkeybars on the school playground
      but
      he was definitely <u>not</u> afraid of Me
                      or God
                or Forever.

We sat facing each other in silence
      I pondering his request
           He quite fascinated with all
                the celestial machinery around us.
      It was rare indeed for so young a fellow
          to seek the final rebirth of resurrection.

"You understand young man that such a thing requires
          a great deal of difficult work," I said.
Experience had shown me that
      in such cases they will usually falter,
        accept some trinket or other,
    and be on about their Lawful Purpose.

<u>The candidate can only work within law-conformable
limits to escape the Law of Nature:</u>
        <u>for the resurrection of even one
           is already outside the Law.</u>

This ancient formulation echoed its reproach
                              through my mind
            and I again tried to dissuade the boy.
"The way to the Sea of Rebirth is uncomfortable,
                painful. You may get lost and never
      find it; in any case you can never return."

At times the boy pretended to be a man
                  adopting a certain swagger
                        and acting the sage:
                              a child's game.
            But he was not acting altogether.

"What you say is true. But the Sea of Rebirth is forever."
                                    So!
                  had he seen the Promise?
            I showed it to him, and followed his eyes
                  as they stopped with each word.

A man may be born, but in order to be
                  born he must first die,
and in order to die he must first awaken.

                  Then the boy laughed
            and at that moment I was convinced
                        he knew its meaning.

There could be no doubt -
            for of all the men and women and children
                  ever to pass this place
                        and read the Promise
                  only a few had laughed . . .
      most could only cry, and collapse into a
                        deeper sleep.

Chapter Twenty-three
Final Judgment

I called through your door,
"The mystics are gathering
in the street. Come out!"

"Leave me alone.
I'm sick."

"I don't care if you're dead!"
Jesus is here, and he wants
To resurrect somebody!"[91]

Living consciously. That seemed to be what all these lessons were about. When I can be conscious in my life, everything around me benefits. Not through effort on my part, or sacrifice, but as a direct byproduct of my fulfilling my purpose. Everyone passing by the lotus flower is uplifted by its fragrance. Everyone passing by the sequoia tree breathes in the oxygen it has exhaled. Everyone who encounters Mountain Elk is inspired by his great stamina, and Butterfly by her life story. The lotus and sequoia, Mountain Elk and Butterfly cannot help but reach their potential, for they are already perfectly unique expressions of the seed from which they sprouted. But humans, you and I, inherit a birthright that offers choice, whether consciously or unconsciously made.

Horse's lesson, and the profound parchment he conveyed to me consumed my attention for many days and weeks. I yearned for the stamina to persevere, even when I felt tired, discouraged, and overwhelmed. I wanted so much to believe that I was legitimately in the process of transforming, of completing my metamorphosis, of liberating from the confines of my cocoon and opening to the vast open spaces. I sought not just to conquer my shortcomings and impose a higher order on myself, but to become something new. And I was quite certain that the something new would be an expansion to incorporate all that came before. I longed for resurrection.

Butterfly returned to inspire me. *Human strengths are inevitably a two-act play involving plummeting descents and soaring heights. This awareness requires that we penetrate more deeply the ironies, paradoxes, and contradictions that are essential features of how we are ennobled.*[92] I understood clearly Butterfly's meaning, that the journey of transformation is never-ending, endlessly expanding. I felt the warmth of immense gratitude in my heart, and the soft comfort of growing peace of mind. I observed the world with *soft eyes*,[93] aware of everything while preoccupied with nothing.

All of creation is a two-act play.[94] *Human death is also a two-act play.* Remaining invisible to me, speaking through the threshold of that interdimensional GPS doorway, Crow spoke to me. *If you succeed in remaining present when your body dies, and have a Good Medicine death, you will triumph over the memory demons and advance through the next Gate. If you miss out on a Good Medicine death when the body dies, you face a second death because you forget who you are. The memory demons, those marauding unburied dead, dominate and greatly limit the choices of what comes next.* Crow seemed almost apologetic about speaking such harsh realities. Yet she exuded confidence about the wonderful opportunity available to anyone who prepares for the moment by giving a decent burial to their unburied dead, retrieving the fragments of essence from witness protection, and living preoccupied with nothing. Then one is eager and ready upon the first death to accept salvation from the second death when it is offered.[95]

These lessons were embodied in my mother's dying. She lived with my wife and I for the final two years of her life, years ninety-eight and ninety-nine. As she approached her last breath, having taken no food or water for a week, I recognized the journey she was on. My lessons had come full circle, from my vision quest to hers. The process of dying is a grand *hanblecheyapi*, or vision quest. Dying, she offered everything she had, her very life, crying for a vision. She journeyed up on the mountain to pray and commune with the Creator, lamenting to realize her oneness with all things, to know that all things are her relatives, and to seek knowledge of the Creator.

For the vision quest of dying, many people serve as *wichasha waken*: the caregivers, hospice workers, medical personnel, spiritual advisors, and most of all the family. And as my dying mother reached a Good Medicine death, all these prayed together, "Oh, Grandfather, *Wakan-Tanka*, today you have helped us. You have been merciful to this woman by giving her knowledge and a path which she may follow. You have made her people happy, and all the beings that move in the universe are rejoicing."

And on her death an auspicious honor was bestowed by Owl, come to recognize a fallen warrior. But this time the owl was not sitting unseen in dark trees nearby, but rather was serenading from within me. For the second time, black owl stepped inside of me, and this time brought liberation from the fear of becoming lost and of dying, equanimity to the agitation of a restless mind, and strength to overcome any tendency to torpor.

Somehow I was able to continue to experience this state of immense gratitude in my heart, and growing peace of mind while sitting on the porch or in the meadow, driving through town or working with students, spilling milk or studying scriptures. And, with the sense of being on the verge of blending with the universal, I discovered one more parchment. It was in the air, and drifted down to where I sat one morning, softly like a feather, free of the gravity of the mundane world. This parchment was barely visible in the bright sunlight.

There is no doubt now: we have discovered
                              another system, a new way.
             A passage in an ancient diary.

Many there are who never die, and so
                    remain in Death forever.
             Concern yourself not with these; leave
                    the dead to bury their dead.

Our goal is at hand.
                    Passing through the Mountain Gate
             not one of us knew what lie ahead
                    and as
                              one by one
                    we entered the Valley
             disappeared the delusion of separateness forever.

And appeared to us a scene
                    in shades of brilliance.
             The quiet sea
                    great mountains all around
             and adrift on the calm waters
                    open and empty caskets.

The fourth dimension. The Fifth Kingdom.

We named our new home the Sea of Rebirth
              though others there called it by other names.

First impressions yield with familiarity
                        but here exists
                  only one perspective:
            perpetual unfoldment,
                  surrender of the personal,
                        proclaim and praise all that is.

We have worked here now
                        for what used to be eternity
                  and continually the quiet deepens,
            and we arise from our open womb-caves.

            The quiet sea
                        celebrates its children
                  for their final liberation
            and echoing over timeless waters
                        comes
            the triumph of emancipation.

For the ceaseless energy flows among us
                        from the most brilliant
                  sunrise evermore

Chapter Twenty-four
The World

Someone once asked the Buddha, "How do we know that you are enlightened?" And he touched the earth and said, "Earth is my witness."

I am now among you again, in a new form. Having learned a little more about life and the great beyond, I returned to continue my own unfoldment and to accompany you in yours. We are in this together, you know, this perpetual unfoldment. My new form you might not recognize. Some may call it angel, although angels are a lot more human than you would guess. Of course, humans are a lot more angelic than you would guess, too.

So I leave you with a *terma* of your own, profoundly hopeful that it might be as helpful to you as all those that blessed me.

And by the way, did you hear my friend Rumi demand, "Roar, lion of the heart, and tear me open." And Hawk describe those passions of the heart as "lifeblood," and Owl explain that the bloody, smoky passions of wrath, jealousy, lust and greed originate not from the heart but from the dark, impenetrable Under World, through the doorway of the liver, and that these fragments of unlived life, the unburied dead deserve a thoughtful burial. Have you found at the core of your heart a sense of profound, unwavering sadness and joy that comes from being truly open to the world and responding deeply to it?

Did Black Owl's lesson strike home for you, about the aspects of yourself that would limit your development: the fear of becoming lost and of dying, the agitation of a restless mind, the heaviness of torpor and drowsiness that blunts awareness, and the mental laxity in which concentration has no strength?

Did you commune, too, with the grove of Douglas Fir and Cedar trees? Were you listening to Mountain Elk's message? And to Owl's exhortation to "Be attentive! Stay conscious!" especially during the transitional times, the dreamtime, the sleep time, and eventually the dying time? Do you have ears to hear mouse, and turtle, and antelope?

Can you see how the fierce, dark and dangerous Guardians at the outskirts of the conventional world are allies who prepare you, the hero, for your journey? Have the dragons of darkness ever killed and eaten you, forcing you to resurrect in a new form? Have they served you well?

Did you swim Dolphin's lessons, too, playing with the demons in the darkness below to tame them, commandeering the energy of those demons and their guardians for healthy harmonious purposes. Can you accept that in darkness, germination? That transforming darkness into light requires taking the long short way through the wild, the dark and the difficult?

Could you stay present for Raven, appearing out of nowhere to declare the same truths that Dolphin had, that diving to the densely packed depths of that ocean of life force could illuminate and liberate those that had descended there, to sprout up like a lotus to blossom in the clarity above, and then to enter the vast openness, to fly through the sky. The soul, too, Raven insisted, is continually appearing out of and vanishing into concealment, either that of the higher realms and vast openness of the *beyond-the-horizon*, or the lower realms and packed density of the *under-the-ground*. Will you heed Raven's lesson that we cannot separate the fieriness of fire from the warmth of fire, but we can separate fire from smoke to quiet the "smoke detector" in the brain. I thank my friend Raven.

Were you touched by Butterfly humbly offering her story of transformation from egg to larva to cocoon and finally to birth? And are you excited by her pointing out that the journey of transformation is endlessly expanding. Are you awed by Whale, embodiment of the wisdom of the ages, teaching that wisdom requires consistently consolidating all that you know, and pruning it by unlearning what you cannot enact in ceremony and carry in your body? Are you willing to explore your interdimensional GPS, doorway to realms which 'other beings' inhabit?

Does preoccupation with your baggage seem to eclipse your ability to attend to your immediate experience? Have you allowed in the crazy wisdom insinuated by Coyote, the great Trickster, to seize the present moment in all its freshness?

Crow, the Left-Handed Guardian, promised that if you obey the Sacred Law, then at death you die a Good Medicine death. Are you encouraged that our divine inheritance insures defeat for Thanatos, the will to inaction, the thief of self-destiny, the frightening, beguiling and embroiling titan?

Did you hear Horse's promise of something greater contained within your present form? Did you hear the exhortation to elevate everything you encounter within the four kingdoms? Did you understand that, having lived as many, we became individuals, and then, ultimately, the delusion of separateness disappears forever? Did you hear the Heart, the ancient sound of one hand clapping that Raven shared?

Did you know that the first stage of spiritual unfoldment is the conscious recognition of bondage, and that the second comes with the revelation of the fallacy of one's personal separateness? That the third stage is a calm following the storm, a period of quest and search amid the dim light of distant sources, and the fourth stage is the incorporation of the knowledge gained into the bodily organism? Did you know that the fifth stage of spiritual unfoldment is a degree of self-liberation from the limitations of physical matter and circumstances, and that the sixth stage is personal consciousness on the verge of blending with the universal? The seventh stage reflects the great illusion that there is a final destination in the Eternal Dance of Life.[96]

Have you heard the call through your door? Are you willing and ready to be resurrected? Have you discovered the final parchment, transparent and wordless? How can one interpret or capture pure being? See through the transparent parchment.

Endnotes

[1] Jelaluddin Rumi, quoted from *The Debtor Sheikh*, a poem by Rumi in *The Essential Rumi* translated by Coleman Barks with John Moyne, HarperSanFrancisco, 1995, p. 160.

[2] Tenzin Wangyal Rinpoche and Mark Dahlby, *The Tibetan Yogas of Dream and Sleep*, Snow Lion Publications, 1st edition, 1998, p. 160.

[3] Joseph Epes Brown, *The Sacred Pipe: Black Elk's Account of the Seven Rites of the Oglala Sioux*, Penguin Books, 1971, p. 46.

[4] Joseph Epes Brown, *The Sacred Pipe*, p. 59.

[5] Michael Fordham, *The Self and Autism*, Society of Analytical Psychology, 1976. The concept of deintegration is suggested by Michael Fordham (1976) to describe the process in which the self allows a disruption of a previous state of integration while a pattern incorporating new material and new understanding is forming. In normal development, deintegration is "in the service of the ego." That is, the self recognizes on a deep level that in order to grow and develop, it must sometimes "stand aside" to allow a deeper and more expansive self to emerge. Deintegration leads to an expansion of experience, a widening of consciousness, a deepening of self concept, an opening to a new identity, and thus to a new level of integration. Fordham and his colleagues observed the process of deintegration and reintegration in newborn infants within days of birth (1976; Sidoli, 1983).

However, the more cataclysmic and chaotic the disturbance of the status quo, the more regressive will be the individual's reaction and the more it will be experienced as disintegrating to the (fragile) ego. The primary, archetypal images and drives that are activated with deintegration may then be experienced as overwhelming. To defend oneself from the resulting feelings of catastrophic despair, annihilation, and disintegration, the individual develops primary defenses in the unconscious, which Fordham calls *defenses of the self* (1974). When the experience is too traumatic to assimilate, a child fails to reintegrate following deintegration and these primary, archetypal patterns become split off from the person's experience of self and trapped in the body (Sidoli & Blakemore, 2000). The child then becomes less open, more rigidly identified with the current self-concept, and less willing to risk deintegration in the future.

[6] Coleman Barks, "On Bewilderment," *The Essential Rumi*, p. 9.

[7] Tenzin Wangyal Rinpoche, *The Tibetan Yogas of Dream and Sleep*, p. 82.

[8] Alberto Villoldo, "Healing and Shamanism with Alberto Villoldo, Ph.D." Thinking Allowed Interview, available at [http://www.intuition.org/txt/villoldo.htm]

[9] Tenzin Wangyal Rinpoche, *The Tibetan Yogas of Dream and Sleep*.

[10] Olga Kharitidi, *The Master of Lucid Dreams*, Hampton Roads Publishing Company, Re-issue edition, 2001.

[11] Stephen LaBerge, *Lucid Dreaming: A Concise Guide to Awakening in Your Dreams and in Your Life*, Sounds True, Har/Com edition, March 2004.

[12] Thomas Moore, "In conversation with Thomas Moore: The soul's mysteries," in A. A. Simpkinson & C. H. Simpkinson (Eds.), *Soul Work: A Field Guide for Spiritual Seekers*, New York: HarperCollins, 1998, pp. 43-45.

[13] Rumi, "The Lame Goat," *The Essential Rumi*, p. 144.

[14] Howard Schwartz, *Reimagining the Bible: The Storytelling of the Rabbis*, New York: Oxford University Press, 1998.

Rabbi Nachman is said to have seen a dead soul for the first time when he was a child. He prayed to see such a soul, and one did indeed seek him out, terrifying him. Later he was said to have seen many such souls of the dead, and at the end of his life he became the Master of the Field, sought out by thousands of souls for the tikkun, or repair, he could do for their souls. The phrase "Master of the Field" comes from one of Reb Nachman's teachings in which he spoke of a field where souls grow, and how they require a master of the field to repair them. (p. 218-219)

[15] It is common for individuals, especially following a traumatic event, to suddenly forget their own history. This experience is sometimes called fugue state (see Hilgard, 1986; Terr, 1994).

[16] Karen O'brien, "The Thin Place Between Life and Death," *Spirituality & Health*, July/August 2005.

[17] Richard A. Chefetz, "The Paradox of 'Detachment Disorders': Binding-Disruptions of Dissociative Process," *Psychiatry: Interpersonal and Biological Processes*, 67(3), Fall 2004, 246-255.

"The monster under the bed, who we all wish to avoid, is raw, bloody Fear. This is the engine that drives dissociation of self. Sometimes it is fear of betrayal, sometimes humiliation, sometimes even fear and disavowal of one's own rage. Often it is a bit of all of these and more. These Fears are painful, lonely children, lost in a complex world, emotionally invalidated, with no place to go in a frightened, disorganized, and contradictory emotional space." (p. 254)

[18] Stephen Larsen, *The Shaman's Doorway*, Rochester, VT: Inner Traditions, pp. 23-24.

Donald E. Kalsched, "Archetypal affect, anxiety and defence in patients who have suffered early trauma," in Ann Casement (Ed.), *Post-Jungians Today: Key Papers in Contemporary Analytical Psychology*, 83-102, London: Routledge, 1998.

The archaic defense of splitting is an anti-embodiment factor working "against the natural process through which the personal spirit embodies - a process Winnicott (1970: 261-70) called 'indwelling' or 'personalization'.

Winnicott envisioned this as that slow process whereby the mother constantly introduces and re-introduces the baby's mind and body to each other (ibid.: 271). In trauma there is a reversal of indwelling, a splitting of affect from image and the corresponding splitting off of the personal spirit from mind/body unity and back into the 'psychoid' realm where, we might imagine, it remains until embodiment is possible." (p. 89)

[19] Rainier Maria Rilke

[20] James Hillman, "Commentary" to *Kundalini: The Evolutionary Energy in Man* by Gopi Krishna, Boston, MA: Shambhala, 1971, p. 133.

[21] Carl Jung, *Man and His Symbols*, Garden City, NY: Doubleday, 1964, p. 161. "As a result of some psychic upheaval whole tracts of our being can plunge back into the unconscious and vanish from the surface for years and decades . . . disturbances caused by affects are known technically as phenomena of dissociation, and are indicative of a psychic split" (Jung, 1934, para. 286). This phenomenon of fragmented identity can, then, result in what Jung referred to as complexes. Jung described such traumatic complexes as "autonomous splinter psyches," fragments which became split off.

[22] Rumi, quoted from "An Awkward Comparison," in *The Essential Rumi* translated by Coleman Barks with John Moyne, p. 177.

[23] John Welwood, *Toward a Psychology of Awakening*, Boston, MA: Shambhala, 2000, p.170.

[24] Jamie Sams & David Carson. *Medicine Cards: The Discovery of Power through the Ways of Animals*, pp. 57-58.

[25] Edward Whitmont, Jungian analyst quoted in *The Shaman's Doorway* by Stephen Larsen, p. 111.

[26] Irini Rockwell, *The Five Wisdom Energies*, Boston, MA: Shambhala, 2002, p. 24.

[27] Carl Jung, *The Psychology of Kundalini Yoga: Notes of the Seminar Given in 1932 by C. G. Jung*, Sonu Shamdasani (Ed.), Bollingen Series XCIX, Princeton, NJ: Princeton University Press, 1996. In a series of lectures in 1932, Jung said, "There are plenty of people who are not yet born. They seem to be all here, they walk about – but as a matter of fact, they are not yet born, because they are behind a glass wall, they are in the womb. They are in the world only on parole and are soon to be returned to the pleroma where they started originally. They have not formed a connection with this world; they are suspended in the air; they are neurotic, living the provisional life. They say, 'I am now living on such-and-such a condition. If my parents behave according to my wishes, I stay. But if it should happen that they do something I don't like, I pop off.' You see, that is the provisional life, a conditioned life, the life of somebody who is still connected by an umbilical cord as thick as a ship's rope to the pleroma, the archetypal world of splendor. Now, it is most important that you should be born; you ought to come into this world –

otherwise you cannot realize the self, and the purpose of this world has been missed. Then you must simply be thrown back into the melting pot and be born again (pp. 28-29).

[28] Paul Foster Case, *The Tarot: A Key to the Wisdom of the Ages*, New York: Macoy Publishing Company, 1947, p. 159.

[29] Tenzin Wangyal Rinpoche. *The Tibetan Yogas of Dream and Sleep.*

[30] Anonymous. *The Life of Milarepa: A New Translation from the Tibetan* by Lobsang P. Lhalungpa, Penguin, 1992, p. 113.

[31] Carl G. Jung, *Memories, Dreams, Reflections*, New York: Random House, 1961, p. 225.

[32] John Davis, "Reflections on Ecopsychology," *Association of Humanistic Psychology Perspective*, 9-11, Feb/Mar 2007. Davis identifies three insights at the core of ecopsychology, which is a relatively new branch of the science of psychology. The first is that humans are connected to the natural world in a profound and emotionally potent way. Nature is not a danger to be controlled or a commodity to be used. Ecopsychology offers two metaphors for human relationship with nature: nature as family (sibling or parent as in Mother Earth and Brother Coyote, and nature as Home, i.e., where a family lives) and nature as self (the Earth as an organism of which we are parts, and we hold the natural world as a larger psyche which incorporates our individual psyches).

The second insight is that the illusion of a disconnection of humans from nature has negative consequences, both for the environment and for our own mental health.

The third insight is that a reconnection is possible. Toward this end, ecopsychology supports a wide range of practices for connecting directly with the natural world: awareness practices that incorporate the natural world, ecotherapy, wilderness therapy, wilderness-based rites of passage, nature-based ritual and shamanic practices, and environmental restoration based on the view that as we heal the Earth, we heal ourselves.

[33] Ralph Metzner, *The Unfolding Self: Varieties of Transformational Experience*, Novato, CA: Origin Press, 1998, p. 73.

[34] Pir Vilayat Inayat Khan, "In conversation with Pir Vilayat Inayat Khan: Nitty-gritty spirituality," in A. A. Simpkinson & C. H. Simpkinson (Eds.), *Soul Work: A Field Guide for Spiritual Seekers*, 333-337, New York: HarperCollins, 1998, p. 334.

[35] The Under World, or Lower World, the individual's Lower Unconscious, consists of all the psychologically damaging experiences of every developmental age, what Firman and Gila (1997) call the *primal wounds*. The Lower Unconscious also includes the collective lower unconscious, what Vaughan (1986) calls the *transpersonal shadow*. A repression barrier operates to keep these identities out of awareness, separated from the whole Self,

protecting the self-interests of the ego. Serving to repress the Lower Unconscious are shame, fear, loneliness, unworthiness, pain, abandonment, and spiritual isolation.

[36] Dori Laub, "Truth and testimony: The process and the struggle," in C. Caruth (Ed.), *Trauma: Explorations in Memory*, 61-75, Baltimore, MD: Johns Hopkins University Press, 1995. She observes, "The loss of the capacity to be a witness to oneself . . . is perhaps the true meaning of annihilation, for when one's history is abolished one's identity ceases to exist as well" (p. 67).

[37] Jamie Sams & David Carson. *Medicine Cards: The Discovery of Power through the Ways of Animals*, p. 45.

[38] John Welwood, *Toward a Psychology of Awakening*, p.189.

[39] Pema Chodron, *Awakening Loving-Kindness*, Boston, MA: Shambhala Publications, 1996, p. 83.

[40] Carl G. Jung, "Commentary on 'The secret of the golden flower'," in *Alchemical Studies* (*Collected Works*: 13, pp.1-55), Princeton: Princeton University Press, 1967, paragraph 54.

[41] Rollin McCraty, Raymond Trevor Bradley, & Dana Tomasino, "The Resonant Heart," *Noetic Sciences Shift* Issue 5, December 2004.

". . . as pulsing waves of energy radiate out from the heart, they interact with organs and other structures. The waves encode or record the features and dynamic activity of these structures in patterns of energy waveforms that are distributed throughout the body. In this way, the encoded information acts to *in-form* (literally, *give shape to*) the activity of all bodily functions--to coordinate and synchronize processes in the body as a whole."

". . . the heart's electromagnetic field can transmit information between people. We have been able to measure an exchange of heart energy between individuals up to five feet apart. We have also found that one person's brain waves can actually synchronize to another person's heart."

". . . both the heart and brain receive and respond to information about a future event *before the event actually happens*. Even more surprising was our finding that the heart appears to receive this "intuitive" information before the brain."

[42] Daniel Goleman, "Neural Wifi: Emotions are more contagious than you think," *Psychotherapy Networker*, Nov/Dec 2006, pp. 60-66.

"When two people interact face to face, contagion spreads via multiple neural circuits operating in parallel within each person's brain. These systems for emotional contagion traffic in the entire range of feeling, from sadness and anxiety to joy.

Moments of contagion represent a remarkable neural event: the formation between two brains of a functional link, a feedback loop that crosses the skin-and-skull barrier between bodies. In systems terms, during this linkup brains 'couple,' with the output of one becoming input to drive the workings of the other, for the time being forming what amounts to an interbrain circuit. When two entities are connected in a feedback loop, as the first changes, so does the second" (p. 62).

Daniel Stern concludes that our nervous systems "are constructed to be captured by the nervous systems of others, so that we can experience others as if from within their skin" (p. 64).

". . . laughter may be the shortest distance between two brains" (p. 65).

". . . 'memes,' ideas that spread from mind to mind, much as emotions do. The notion of a meme was modeled on that of a gene: an entity that replicates itself by getting passed on from person to person.

Memes with particular power, like 'democracy' or 'cleanliness,' lead us to act in a specific way; they are ideas with impact. Some memes naturally oppose others, and when they do, those memes are at war, a battle of ideas.

Memes seem to gather power from the low road, through their association with strong emotions" (p. 65).

[43] Robert Scaer, "The Precarious Present: Why Is It So Hard to Stay in the Present Moment?" *Psychotherapy Networker*, Nov/Dec 2006, pp. 48-53, 67.

"How often do we find ourselves ruminating about this or that familiar resentment or well-worn worry? How often do we truly notice where we are, whom we're with, or what's actually happening--that is, experience our own precious moments? It's as though some dark, implacable entity invades our minds and bodies and fills them to the brim, leaving little space for pleasure in our aliveness, much less for growth or healing. That entity, I believe, is the total body-mind experience of a past trauma" (p.51).

[44] Rollin McCraty, Mike Atkinson, & Raymond Trevor Bradley, "Electrophysiological Evidence of Intuition: Part 2. A System-Wide Process?" *The Journal of Alternative and Complementary Medicine*, 10(2), pp. 325–336, 2004.

McCraty and his team of researchers have independently replicated and extended previous research documenting pre-stimulus responses, that is information about a future event *before the event actually happens*. It appears that the heart and brain, together, are involved in the receiving, processing and decoding of such intuitive information. Their research presents compelling evidence that the body's perceptual apparatus (the heart and brain and possibly other bodily systems) is continuously *scanning the future*.

[45] Carl Jung quoted by Donald E. Kalsched, "Archetypal affect, anxiety and defence in patients who have suffered early trauma," p. 100.

[46] David Abram, *The Spell of the Sensuous: Perception and Language in a More-Than-Human World*, New York: Vintage Books, 1996, pp. 213-221.

[47] Pema Chodron, quoting a well-known Buddhist saying.

[48] Genesis 1:1 and 2. King James Version of the Holy Bible.

[49] Abraham Maslow's Hierarchy of Needs (1943, 1954): Lower level, more basic needs must be met before higher level needs can be addressed. They are, in order from lowest to highest:

1) Physiological: hunger, thirst, bodily comforts, etc.;

2) Safety/security: out of danger;

3) Belongingness and Love: affiliate with others, be accepted; and

4) Esteem: to achieve, be competent, gain approval and recognition

Subsequently added to the hierarchy of needs (1968, 1971):

5) Cognitive: to know, to understand, and explore;

6) Aesthetic: symmetry, order, and beauty;

7) Self-actualization: to find self-fulfillment and realize one's potential; and

8) Transcendence: to help others find self-fulfillment and realize their potential.

[50] Olga Kharitidi, *Master of Lucid Dreams*. The shamanic wisdom of Siberia and Central Asia as described in *Master of Lucid Dreams*, refers to the positive power of subjugated energies from the Lower World:

"The memory space is populated by images. The memory demons can be seen as images too, but they have much more conscious energy in them than usual memories. And exactly because of that, when they are seen and transformed, they don't disappear, but change the quality of their energy and start serving you after you conquer them. This is how shamans obtain the most powerful spirit helpers. Many believe that shamans get their helpers through transmission from older shamans. This is true.

But somewhere along the line, those spirit helpers were memory demons, who were transformed and subjugated by a shaman who turned them into obedient servants. It is a matter of the transformation of psychic energy. Lucid dreams and shamanic journeys are the best states for that." (p. 147)

The Ancient Hebrew wisdom conveyed through the Kabbalah discusses two potential methods of attempting to bring the material nature of the body and the animal soul into sacred service: *Itkafia* (conquest) and *It'hapcha* (transformation). Conquest requires a battle, and is achieved through subjugating and subordinating the inclination for self-indulgence or self-destruction. Transformation is the process whereby spiritual ignorance and self-indulgence are lovingly reformulated into selfless service of G-d. In both cases the otherwise obstructing psychic energy is, hopefully, brought into service.

Carl S. Hale, "Psychocatabolism and the dark night of the self," *Journal of Humanistic Psychology*, 32(1), 65-89, 1992. Hale discusses the "dark night of the self", calling it "the descent of the ego into its own dark matrix, the source of consciousness, identity, and awareness - the existential and transpersonal unconscious" (p. 65). Hale emphasizes that it is from this realm that the innate energies of healing are released.

[51] Gary Toub. "Taoism and Self-Actualization," available online at http://www.cgjungpage.org/index.php?option=com_content&task=view&id=149&Itemid=40.

This can be seen as a Taoist view. Taoism is based on thousands of years of observing patterns of change and transformation in nature. The Tao has been called the Way, or Main Road, and is seen as describing a way of being and course of action that is in harmony with the wisdom of the Self. Its meaning corresponds to Don Juan's "path with heart" (Castaneda, 1968) and Joseph Campbell's (1988) "following your bliss."

According to Chung-yuan (1963), the oldest form of the Chinese ideograph for Tao consists of three basic parts, representing a human head, a human foot, and a road. The character for the head (*shou*) is connected with heaven, the sun, and masculine, yang energy, while the foot (*ch'o*) is associated with the earth and feminine, yin energy (Bolen, 1979). The foot and road, considered as a unit, allude to stepwise movement along a path, or as Watts (1975, p. 39) puts it, "rhythmic movement." This suggests a type of movement where pauses are taken to think or reflect before the next step is taken.

[52] John Selby, *Kundalini Awakening: A Gentle Guide to Chakra Activation and Spiritual Growth*, New York: Bantam Books, 1992, p. 147.

[53] Rumi, "What Shall I Be," in Idries Shah, *The Way of the Sufi*, New York: Dutton, 1970, p. 107.

[54] Joseph Campbell, *Myths to Live By*, New York: Viking Penguin, 1972, pp. 208-209.

[55] Jamie Sams & David Carson, *Medicine Cards: The Discovery of Power through the Ways of Animals*, pp. 73-74.

[56] Paul Reps, *Zen Flesh Zen Bones*, Boston, MA: Tuttle Publishing, Reprint edition, 1998, pp. 33-34.

[57] Jon Kabat-Zinn, quoted in "The Power of Paying Attention" by Mary Sykes Wylie & Rich Simon, *Psychotherapy Networker*, Nov/Dec 2004.

[58] Mary Sykes Wylie, "The Limits of Talk," *Psychotherapy Networker*, Jan/Feb 2004.

Remembering a traumatic event shuts down the left frontal cortex of the brain, the area that allows rational understanding and the ability to speak about what is happening. But those same memories light up areas of the right hemisphere associated with emotional states and autonomic arousal. The amygdala becomes agitated with trauma, even remembered trauma.

[59] Fabrice Midal, *Chogyam Trungpa: His Life and Vision*, Boston: Shambhala Publications, 2004, p.75.

[60] Jamie Sams & David Carson. *Medicine Cards: The Discovery of Power through the Ways of Animals*, pp. 202-203.

[61] Francis Crick & G. Mitchison. "The functions of dream sleep." *Nature*, 304, 1983, 111-114.

These researchers propose that the function of dream (REM) sleep is to remove certain undesirable modes of interaction in networks of cells in the cerebral cortex. It is suggested that in viviparous mammals, the cortical system is subjected to unwanted or "parasitic" modes of behavior, which arise as the system is disturbed either by the growth of the brain or by the modifications produced by experience. Such modes are detected and suppressed by a special mechanism that operates during REM sleep and has the character of an active process that is the opposite of learning. It is argued that any purely psychological theory, such as Freud's, cannot explain the large amount of REM sleep in the womb; any purely developmental theory must account for the substantial amount of REM sleep in adult life. The authors believe that their theory accounts for both of these occurrences and is compatible with the hallucinoid nature of REM dreams. It is postulated that some forms of schizophrenia are caused by a defect in the reverse learning process.

[62] Helen Crawford, "Brain dynamics and hypnosis: Attentional and disattentional processes," *International Journal of Clinical and Experimental Hypnosis*, 42(3), 1994, 204-232.

[63] Mihaly Csikszentmihalyi, *Flow: The Psychology of Optimal Experience*, New York: HarperPerrenial, 1990.

"Mild mystical experiences" have been studied by Csikszentmihalyi, who calls them "flow": a joyous and creative total involvement with life. His research has shown that these experiences occur to people in the course of many surprisingly commonplace activities: working, dancing, climbing a mountain, gardening. For some people, inner anxiety and self-consciousness disappear when they become deeply engaged in such pursuits. "What slips below the threshold of awareness," he says, "is the concept of self, the information we use to represent to ourselves who we are" (p. xi). Csikszentmihalyi also has found evidence of a range of experiences in which people's identities seem to merge with something else - a sailor with his boat, a violinist with her instrument. These mild mystical experiences are characterized by the fluidity in distinction between self and other and a loss of self-awareness. Csikszentmihalyi has distilled eight components of the experience of *flow*:

1. *engagement in a challenge* for which the person has the necessary skill to excel

2. *absorption* in which one's awareness merges with one's actions

3. *setting of clear goals* that are unambiguous even though they may be complex
4. *presence of feedback* that the goals are being reached
5. *attenuation of one's usual concerns* while one is absorbed in the challenge
6. *opportunity to exercise control*, to be proactively involved
7. *loss of self-awareness* which involves the sense of individuality melting away, and is sometimes accompanied by an *identification or merging with one's environment*
8. *freedom from the uniform ordering of time*, with hours passing by unnoticed.

[64] Michael Winkelman, *Shamanism: The Neural Ecology of Consciousness and Healing*, Westport, CT: Bergin and Garvey, 2000.

[65] Louise Danielle Palmer, "This is Your Brain Praying," *Spirituality & Health*, Jan/Feb 2004.

[66] Niels C. Rattenborg, C. J. Amlaner, & S. L. Lima. "Behavioral, neurophysiological, and evolutionary perspectives on unihemispheric sleep." *Neuroscience and Biobehavioral Reviews*, 24(8), 2000, 817-842.

[67] Franklyn Sills, *Craniosacral Biodynamics: The Breath of Life, Biodynamics, and Fundamental Skills*, Berkeley, CA: North Atlantic Books, 2001, p. 63.

[68] Jayne Gackenbach. In F. J. Varela (Ed.), *Sleeping, Dreaming, and Dying: An exploration of Consciousness with the Dalai Lama,* Boston, MA: Wisdom Publications, 1997.

Gackenbach suggests that waking, sleeping (non REM), and dreaming (REM) "emerge out of a pure consciousness, a silent void. Where each state meets the next there's a little gap, in which Travis postulates that everybody very briefly experiences transcendental consciousness. When we go from sleeping to dreaming, or from dreaming to waking, these little gaps or junction points occur" (p. 109). The research she refers to is from Fred Travis (1994; Travis & Pearson, 2000) in which he has documented with EEG research a common experience available at these transitions, an underlying field of transcendental consciousness, and shown that the same experience is achieved in certain meditation states. The following figure, from his 1994 article, graphically represents his findings:

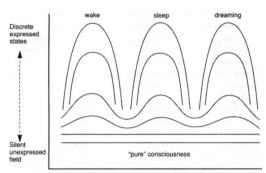

[69] David S. Shannahoff-Khalsa, *Kundalini Yoga Meditation: Techniques Specific for Psychiatric Disorders, Couples Therapy, and Personal Growth*, New York: W. W. Norton & Company, 2006.

[70] Idries Shah, "Short Cuts," in *Reflections*, Baltimore, MD: Penguin Books, 1971, p. 127.

[71] Ernest Rossi, "Altered states of consciousness in everyday life: The ultradian rhythms," in B. Wolman and M. Ullman (Eds.), *Handbook of States of Consciousness*, New York: Van Nostrand Reinhold, 1986.
The normal integration of the waking and the dream modes is illustrated in Rossi's (1986) research on the ultradian rhythms and the sleep-dream-waking cycles, which showed that dreamlike periods and mentation also occur during the waking mode. The information processing of dreams also occasionally intrudes on waking consciousness.

[72] Thomas Hora, "The process of existential psychotherapy," *Psychiatric Quarterly*, 34, 1960, 495-504.

[73] Jamie Sams & David Carson. *Medicine Cards: The Discovery of Power through the Ways of Animals*, pp. 133-135.

[74] Carl Jung. He described personality fragments which became split off as "autonomous splinter psyches," and called them traumatic complexes. In fact, Jung refers to our tendency to identify with a complex as an instance of *possession* (Jung, 1959, p. 122). One identity, or complex, hijacks the whole confederation of identities for a moment or two before another takes over. "Everyone knows that people have complexes," Jung wrote, but "what is not so well known … is that complexes can have us" (Jung, 1964, p. 161). See also endnote 21.

[75] Mara Sidoli & Phyllis Blakemore, *When the Body Speaks: The Archetypes in the Body*, London: Routledge, 2000, p. 91:
"According to Jung, bodily experiences relating to instinctual discharges constitute the most deeply unconscious psychic elements, which can never become completely conscious."

[76] Mark Epstein, *Thoughts Without a Thinker: Psychotherapy from a Buddhist Perspective*, New York: Basic Books, 1995, pp. 80-81.

[77] Peretz Lavie, "Sleep-Wake as a Biological Rhythm," *Annual Review of Psychology*, Vol. 52, 2001, 277-303.

The hypothalamus in the brain regulates the sleep gate. The hypothalamus is an important control center for many physiological functions. It controls the autonomic nervous system, regulates the pituitary gland, and secretes several hormones and other chemical factors. The hypothalamus appears to be the center for the learned control of autonomic functions that occur during relaxation and biofeedback training.

[78] Michael I. Posner & Marcus E. Raichle, *Images of Mind*, New York: Scientific American Library, 1994, p. 175:

"Researchers at the National Institutes of Health have confirmed that vigilance increases activation in the right frontal lobe. In addition, they have found that as this activation rises, the anterior cingulate is quiet. If the anterior cingulate plays a role in target detection, its lack of activation makes sense. In tasks where one needs to suspend activity while waiting for infrequent signals, it is important not to carry out any mental activity that might interfere with detecting the external event. Subjectively, one feels empty headed, as one tries to avoid any stray thoughts."

[79] Rick Strassman, *DMT Spirit Molecule: A Doctor's Revolutionary Research into the Biology of Near-Death and Mystical Experiences*, Park Street Press, 2001.

Pineal gland activity increases in darkness (and during winter), and decreases in the light (and in summer). It manufactures melatonin, which plays a critical role in regulating the sleep-wake cycle. It also manufactures dimethyltryptamine, which plays a major role in the visionary activity of dreams, near-death experiences and other mystical states. It distorts space and time perception, awareness of being a human ego/self, and has the uncanny tendency to open the door of emergence into an alien world. Dr. Strassman has proposed that DMT is produced within the pineal gland of the human brain. Strassman also holds a theory that massive amounts of DMT are released from the pineal gland prior to death or near death, explaining the near-death experience phenomenon.

He suggests that the spirit molecule, a "biological basis for spiritual experience," elicits, with reasonable reliability, certain psychological states we consider "spiritual." These are feelings of extraordinary joy, timelessness, and a certainty that what we are experiencing is "more real than real." Such a substance may lead us to an acceptance of the coexistence of opposites, such as life and death, good and evil; a knowledge that consciousness continues after death; a deep understanding of the basic unity of all phenomena; and a sense of wisdom or love pervading all existence.

Equally important is that DMT, the spirit molecule, occurs in our bodies. We produce it naturally. Our brain seeks it out, pulls it in, and readily digests it.

J. C. Callaway, "A proposed mechanism for the visions of dream sleep," *Medical Hypotheses*, 26, 1988, 119-124.

Medical researcher J. C. Callaway, suggested in 1988 that naturally occurring DMT might be connected with visual dream phenomena, where levels of DMT in the brain are elevated.

[80] Michael A. Thalbourne, "Relation between transliminality and openness to experience," *Psychological Reports*, 86, 2000, 909-910.

Michael Thalbourne has thoroughly researched *transliminality*. This is the tendency for psychological material (imagery, ideation, affect, and perception) to cross thresholds into or out of consciousness with ease. Some people are more transliminal than others. Thalbourne's research (2000) documents that people who are highly transliminal also score high on the personality dimension of openness to experience (McCrae, 1994). The transitional state always requires some element of surrender, allowing a dissolution of the "everyday ego consciousness" beliefs in absoluteness and solidity of material existence, beliefs in separateness and boundariedness between oneself and everything else, beliefs in the linearity of time and fixity of space. Interestingly, there is a clear developmental antecedent to adult transliminality: childhood trauma. Survivors of childhood abuse score significantly higher than others on these aspects of transliminality: the altered state of cosmic enlightenment, fantasy proneness, special wisdom, sensing an evil presence, absorption in nature or art, a transformative state of consciousness, mystical experience, hyperesthesia, and the sense of gaining or losing energy. "Childhood trauma seems predictive of the broad domain of transliminality" (Thalbourne & Crawley, 2003, p. 692).

[81] Rabbi Nachman of Bratslav, quoted in Arthur Green, *Tormented Master: The Life and Spiritual Quest of Rabbi Nahman of Bratslav*, Jewish Lights Publications, 1992, p. 148.

[82] Fabrice Midal, *Chogyam Trungpa: His Life and Vision*, p. 364.

[83] Jamie Sams & David Carson, *Medicine Cards: The Discovery of Power through the Ways of Animals*, pp. 89-91.

[84] Chogyam Trungpa, *Crazy Wisdom*, Boston: Shambhala Publications, 1991, p. 84.

[85] David Hartman and Diane Zimberoff, "The existential approach in Heart-Centered therapies," *Journal of Heart-Centered Therapies*, 6(1), 2003, 3-46. The authors offer the following five principles of an existential approach to healing, transformation, and to life itself:

1. Meaning in life is found in the living of each moment.

2. Passionate commitment to a way of life, to one's purpose and one's relationships, is the highest form of expression of one's humanity.
3. All human beings have freedom of choice and responsibility for our choices.
4. Openness to experience allows for the greatest possible expansion of personal expression.
5. In the ever-present face of death itself, we find the deepest commitment to life itself.

[86] Jeremy Hayward, *Sacred World: A Guide to Shambhala Warriorship in Daily Life*, New York: Bantam New Age, 1995, p. 124.

[87] John Selby, *Kundalini Awakening: A Gentle Guide to Chakra Activation and Spiritual Growth*, p. 157.

[88] James H. Austin, "Consciousness evolves when the self dissolves," *Journal of Consciousness Studies*, 7(11-12), 2000, 209-230.

[89] David Hartman and Diane Zimberoff, "*De*integrate, *Dis*integrate, *Un*integrate: A Buddhist Perspective in Heart-Centered Therapies," *Journal of Heart-Centered Therapies*, 6(2), 2003, 27-87.

The authors summarize the principles of living in the Aikido way, which may be a good analogy for living with such a peace of mind:
1. Expect nothing. Be ready for anything.
2. Observe everything while being preoccupied with nothing.
3. Openness to the unknown and unknowable, to incompatibilities and paradox
4. Spontaneity – saying yes to life
5. Less judging and prejudging
6. Non-defensiveness
7. Surrender
8. Relaxation, absence of excess tension
9. Vulnerability – loss of reactivity
10. Certainty in one's intuition
11. Letting go of attachments
12. Continuity of self
13. Non-judgmental perception of self and others
14. Integrity of spirituality
15. Nonattachment to role, image, or identity
16. Increased awareness of subtle energies inside and outside of the body.
17. Humility
18. Forgiveness
19. Completion (no unfinished business)
20. Compassion and selfless service
21. Sacredness of everyday experience

[90] Fabrice Midal, *Chogyam Trungpa: His Life and Vision*, p. 457.

[91] Rumi, An unnamed poem in *The Essential Rumi*, pp. 201-202.

[92] Carol D. Ryff & Burton Singer, "Ironies of the human condition: Well-being and health on the way to mortality," in Lisa G. Aspinwall and Ursula M. Staudinger (Eds.), *A Psychology of Human Strengths: Fundamental Questions and Future Directions for a Positive Psychology*, 271-287. American Psychological Association, 2003, p. 272.

[93] Rod Windle & Michael Samko, "Hypnosis, Ericksonian hypnotherapy, and Aikido," *American Journal of Clinical Hypnosis*, 34(4), 1992, 261-270.

The authors suggest that the attributes of the Aikido state of centering include "soft" eyes (simultaneous use of focus and peripheral vision, which allows one to observe everything while being preoccupied with nothing).

[94] Yanki Tauber, *The Cosmic Twins: a Parshah Overview*, from the Chassidic Masters. Retrieved from the website http://www.chabad.org/parshah/article.asp?AID=35866.

The creation story in the Bible, Genesis 2:7, describes the creation of human beings as occurring in two segments, taking dust from the earth already created to form it into a creature (a body), and then infusing the dust-formed body with the breath of life (a soul).

This twofold process of creation is recounted, not just for man but for the universe itself. Ancient Hebrew wisdom differentiates two successive creations, with the earlier one providing deeply buried treasures for intrepid explorers to find and mine. "Our sages tell us that before G-d created our world, He created an "earlier" state of existence -- the world of *Tohu* ('Chaos'). But this was a world of 'much light and scant vessels'; as a result, the vessels burst and the light escaped. G-d then created 'our' world -- the world of *Tikkun* ('Correction'), constructed with 'broad containers and scant light' that allow it to function and endure" (Tauber). *Light* is the Kabbalistic term for an emanation of Divine energy; *containers* are the Divine forces that channel, define, and focus the light. A soul is a light, while a body is a vessel.

"There was a reason for this 'debacle.' G-d desired that our 'correct' world should be built upon the ruins of Tohu, so that we should delve beneath its surface to unearth the 'sparks of holiness' that are the residue of this primordial world, tap their potent potential, and, ultimately, integrate the two realities, capturing the immense light of Tohu in the broad vessels of Tikkun."

[95] Olga Kharitidi, *Master of Lucid Dreams*, p. 160. She refers to the shamanic wisdom of Siberia and Central Asia regarding death and salvation.

[96] Paul Foster Case. *The Tarot: A Key to the Wisdom of the Ages*, pp. 154-199.

These seven stages of spiritual unfoldment are represented by Tarot major trump cards 15 through 21, as summarized by Case.

There are parallels between this sequential unfoldment and Abraham Maslow's Hierarchy of Needs as he eventually envisioned it, discussed in endnote 49.

References

Abram, David. *The Spell of the Sensuous: Perception and Language in a More-Than-Human World.* New York: Vintage Books, 1996.
Austin, James H. "Consciousness evolves when the self dissolves." *Journal of Consciousness Studies*, 7(11-12), 2000, 209-230.
Barks, Coleman with John Moyne. *The Essential Rumi.* HarperSanFrancisco, 1995.
Bolen, Jean Shinoda. *The Tao of Psychology.* San Francisco: Harper & Row, 1979.
Brown, Joseph Epes. *The Sacred Pipe: Black Elk's Account of the Seven Rites of the Oglala Sioux.* Penguin Books, 1971.
Callaway, J. C. "A proposed mechanism for the visions of dream sleep." *Medical Hypotheses*, 26, 1988, 119-124.
Campbell, Joseph. *Myths to Live By.* New York: Viking Penguin, 1972.
Campbell, Joseph. *The Power of Myth.* New York: Doubleday, 1988.
Case, Paul Foster. *The Tarot: A Key to the Wisdom of the Ages.* New York: Macoy Publishing, 1947.
Castaneda, Carlos. *The Teachings of Don Juan: A Yaqui Way of Knowledge.* Berkeley, CA: University of California Press, 1968.
Chefetz, Richard A. "The paradox of 'Detachment Disorders': Binding-disruptions of dissociative process." *Psychiatry: Interpersonal and Biological Processes*, 67(3), Fall 2004, 246-255.
Chodron, Pema. *Awakening Loving-Kindness.* Boston, MA: Shambhala Publications, 1996.
Chogyam Trungpa. *Crazy Wisdom.* Boston: Shambhala Publications, 1991.
Chung-yuan, C. *Creativity and Taoism.* New York: Harper & Row, 1963.
Crawford, Helen. "Brain dynamics and hypnosis: Attentional and disattentional processes." *International Journal of Clinical and Experimental Hypnosis*, 42(3), 1994, 204-232.
Crick, Francis & G. Mitchison. "The functions of dream sleep." *Nature*, 304, 1983, 111-114.
Csikszentmihalyi, Mihaly. *Flow: The Psychology of Optimal Experience.* New York: HarperPerrenial, 1990.
Davis, John. "Reflections on Ecopsychology." *Association of Humanistic Psychology Perspective*, 9-11, Feb/Mar 2007.

Epstein, Mark. *Thoughts Without a Thinker: Psychotherapy from a Buddhist Perspective*. New York: Basic Books, 1995.

Firman, John & Ann Gila. *The Primal Wound: A Transpersonal View of Trauma, Addiction, and Growth*. Albany, NY: State University of New York Press, 1997.

Fordham, Michael. "Defences of the self." *Journal of Analytical Psychology*, 19(2), 1974.

Fordham, Michael. *The Self and Autism*. London: Society of Analytical Psychology, 1976.

Gackenbach, Jayne. In F. J. Varela (Ed.), *Sleeping, Dreaming, and Dying: An Exploration of Consciousness with the Dalai Lama*. Boston, MA: Wisdom Publications, 1997.

Goleman, Daniel. "Neural Wifi: Emotions are more contagious than you think." *Psychotherapy Networker*, Nov/Dec 2006.

Green, Arthur. *Tormented Master: The Life and Spiritual Quest of Rabbi Nahman of Bratslav*. Jewish Lights Publications, 1992.

Hale, Carl S. "Psychocatabolism and the dark night of the self." *Journal of Humanistic Psychology*, 32(1), 1992, 65-89.

Hartman, David & Diane Zimberoff. "The existential approach in Heart-Centered therapies." *Journal of Heart-Centered Therapies*, 6(1), 2003a, 3-46.

Hartman, David & Diane Zimberoff. "*De*integrate, *dis*integrate, *un*integrate: A Buddhist perspective in Heart-Centered therapies." *Journal of Heart-Centered Therapies*, 6(2), 2003b, 27-87.

Hayward, Jeremy. *Sacred World: A Guide to Shambhala Warriorship in Daily Life*. New York: Bantam New Age, 1995.

Hilgard, Ernest R. *Divided Consciousness: Multiple Controls in Human Thought and Action (expanded ed.)*. New York: Wiley, 1986.

Hillman, James. "Commentary." In *Kundalini: The Evolutionary Energy in Man* by Gopi Krishna, Boston, MA: Shambhala, 1971.

Hora, Thomas. "The process of existential psychotherapy." *Psychiatric Quarterly*, 34, 1960, 495-504.

Jung, Carl G. *The Meaning of Psychology for Modern Man. Collected Works, Vol. 10*. Princeton, NJ: Princeton University Press, 1934.

Jung, Carl G. *The Archetypes and the Collective Unconscious*. Princeton, NJ: Princeton University Press, 1959.

Jung, Carl G. *Memories, Dreams, Reflections*. New York: Random House, 1961.

Jung, Carl G. *Man and His Symbols*. Garden City, NY: Doubleday, 1964.

Jung, Carl G. "Commentary on 'The secret of the golden flower'." In *Alchemical Studies* (*Collected Works*: 13, pp.1-55), Princeton: Princeton University Press, 1967.

Jung, Carl G. *The Psychology of Kundalini Yoga: Notes of the Seminar Given in 1932 by C. G. Jung*, Sonu Shamdasani (Ed.), Bollingen Series XCIX. Princeton, NJ: Princeton University Press, 1996.

Kabat-Zinn, Jon. In "The power of paying attention" by Mary Sykes Wylie & Rich Simon, *Psychotherapy Networker*, Nov/Dec 2004.

Kalsched, Donald E. "Archetypal affect, anxiety and defence in patients who have suffered early trauma." In Ann Casement (Ed.), *Post-Jungians Today: Key Papers in Contemporary Analytical Psychology*, 83-102, London: Routledge, 1998.

Khan, Pir Vilayat Inayat. "In conversation with Pir Vilayat Inayat Khan: Nitty-gritty spirituality." In A. A. Simpkinson & C. H. Simpkinson (Eds.), *Soul Work: A Field Guide for Spiritual Seekers*, 333-337, New York: HarperCollins, 1998.

Kharitidi, Olga. *The Master of Lucid Dreams*. Charlottesville, VA: Hampton Roads Publishing Company, Re-issue edition, 2001.

LaBerge, Stephen. *Lucid Dreaming: A Concise Guide to Awakening in Your Dreams and in Your Life*. Sounds True, Har/Com edition, March 2004.

Larsen, Stephen. *The Shaman's Doorway*. Rochester, VT: Inner Traditions.

Laub, Dori. "Truth and testimony: The process and the struggle." In C. Caruth (Ed.), *Trauma: Explorations in Memory*, 61-75, Baltimore, MD: Johns Hopkins University Press, 1995.

Lavie, Peretz. "Sleep-Wake as a Biological Rhythm." *Annual Review of Psychology*, Vol. 52, 2001, 277-303.

Lhalungpa, Lobsang P. *The Life of Milarepa: A New Translation from the Tibetan*. Penguin, 1992.

Maslow, Abraham. "A theory of human motivation." *Psychological Review*, 50, 1943, 370-396.

Maslow, Abraham H. *Motivation and Personality*. New York: Harper & Row, 1954.

Maslow, Abraham. *Toward a Psychology of Being*, second edition. Princeton, NJ: Van Nostrand, 1968.

Maslow, Abraham. *The Farther Reaches of Human Nature*. New York: Viking, 1971.

McCrae, Robert R. "Openness to experience: Expanding the boundaries of Factor V." *European Journal of Personality*, 8, 1994, 251-272.

McCraty, Rollin, Mike Atkinson, & Raymond Trevor Bradley. "Electrophysiological evidence of intuition: Part 2. A system-wide process?" *The Journal of Alternative and Complementary Medicine*, 10(2), 2004, 325–336.

McCraty, Rollin, Raymond Trevor Bradley, & Dana Tomasino. "The Resonant Heart." *Noetic Sciences Shift*, 5, December 2004.

Metzner, Ralph. *The Unfolding Self: Varieties of Transformational Experience*. Novato, CA: Origin Press, 1998.

Midal, Fabrice. *Chogyam Trungpa: His Life and Vision*. Boston: Shambhala Publications, 2004.

Moore, Thomas. "In conversation with Thomas Moore: The soul's mysteries." In A. A. Simpkinson & C. H. Simpkinson (Eds.), *Soul Work: A Field Guide for Spiritual Seekers*, New York: HarperCollins, 1998.

O'brien, Karen. "The Thin Place between life and death." *Spirituality & Health*, July/August 2005.

Palmer, Louise Danielle. "This is your brain praying." *Spirituality & Health*, Jan/Feb 2004. [Available at http://www.spiritualityhealth.com/NMagazine/articles.php?id=24].

Posner, Michael I. & Marcus E. Raichle. *Images of Mind*. New York: Scientific American Library, 1994.

Rattenborg, Niels C., C. J. Amlaner, & S. L. Lima. "Behavioral, neurophysiological, and evolutionary perspectives on unihemispheric sleep." *Neuroscience and Biobehavioral Reviews*, 24(8), 2000, 817-842.

Reps, Paul. *Zen Flesh Zen Bones*. Boston, MA: Tuttle Publishing, Reprint edition, 1998.

Rockwell, Irini. *The Five Wisdom Energies*. Boston, MA: Shambhala, 2002.

Rossi, Ernest. "Altered states of consciousness in everyday life: The ultradian rhythms." In B. Wolman & M. Ullman (Eds.), *Handbook of States of Consciousness*, New York: Van Nostrand Reinhold, 1986.

Ryff, Carol D. & Burton Singer. "Ironies of the human condition: Well-being and health on the way to mortality." In Lisa G. Aspinwall & Ursula M. Staudinger (Eds.), *A Psychology of Human Strengths: Fundamental Questions and Future Directions for a Positive Psychology*, 271-287, Washington, DC: American Psychological Association, 2003.

Sams, Jamie & David Carson. *Medicine Cards: The Discovery of Power through the Ways of Animals.* Santa Fe, NM: Bear & Company, 1988.

Scaer, Robert. "The precarious present: Why is it so hard to stay in the present moment?" *Psychotherapy Networker*, Nov/Dec 2006, 48-53, 67.

Schwartz, Howard. *Reimagining the Bible: The Storytelling of the Rabbis.* New York: Oxford University Press, 1998.

Selby, John. *Kundalini Awakening: A Gentle Guide to Chakra Activation and Spiritual Growth.* New York: Bantam Books, 1992.

Shannahoff-Khalsa, David S. *Kundalini Yoga Meditation: Techniques Specific for Psychiatric Disorders, Couples Therapy, and Personal Growth.* New York: W. W. Norton & Company, 2006.

Shah, Idries. *The Way of the Sufi.* New York: Dutton, 1970.

Sidoli, Mara. "De-integration and re-integration in the first two weeks of life." *Journal of Analytical Psychology*, 28, 1983, 201-212.

Sidoli, Mara & Phyllis Blakemore. *When the Body Speaks: The Archetypes in the Body.* London: Routledge, 2000.

Sills, Franklyn. *Craniosacral Biodynamics: The Breath of Life, Biodynamics, and Fundamental Skills.* Berkeley, CA: North Atlantic Books, 2001.

Strassman, Rick. *DMT Spirit Molecule: A Doctor's Revolutionary Research into the Biology of Near-Death and Mystical Experiences.* Park Street Press, 2001.

Sykes Wylie, Mary. "The limits of talk." *Psychotherapy Networker*, Jan/Feb 2004.

Sykes Wylie, Mary & Rich Simon. "The power of paying attention." *Psychotherapy Networker*, Nov/Dec 2004.

Toub, Gary. "Taoism and Self-Actualization," available online at http://www.cgjungpage.org/index.php?option=com_content&task=vie w&id=149&Itemid=40.

Tauber, Yanki. *"The Cosmic Twins: a Parshah Overview."* From the Chassidic Masters. Retrieved from the website http://www.chabad.org/parshah/article.asp?AID=35866.

Tenzin Wangyal Rinpoche & Mark Dahlby. *The Tibetan Yogas of Dream and Sleep.* Snow Lion Publications, 1st edition, 1998.

Terr, Lenore. *Unchained Memories: True Stories of Traumatic Memories, Lost and Found.* New York: Basic Books, 1994.

Thalbourne, Michael A. "Relation between transliminality and openness to experience." *Psychological Reports*, 86, 2000, 909-910.

Thalbourne, Michael A. & Susan E. Crawley. "Childhood trauma as a possible antecedent of transliminality." *Psychological Reports*, 93, 2003, 687-694.

Travis, Fred. "The junction point model: A field model of waking, sleeping, and dreaming, relating dream witnessing, the waking/sleeping transition, and Transcendental Meditation in terms of a common psychophysiologic state." *Dreaming*, 4(2), June 1994, 91-104.

Travis, Fred & Craig Pearson. "Pure consciousness: Distinct phenomenological and physiological correlates of 'consciousness itself'." *International Journal of Neuroscience*, 100(1-4), Jan-Feb 2000, 77-89.

Vaughan, Frances. *The Inward Arc: Healing and Wholeness in Psychotherapy and Spirituality*. Boston: New Science Library/Shambhala, 1986.

Villoldo, Alberto. "Healing and Shamanism with Alberto Villoldo, Ph.D." Thinking Allowed Interview, available at [http://www.intuition.org/txt/villoldo.htm].

Watts, Alan. *Tao: The Watercourse Way*. New York: Pantheon Books, 1975.

Welwood, John. *Toward a Psychology of Awakening*. Boston, MA: Shambhala, 2000.

Windle, Rod & Michael Samko. "Hypnosis, Ericksonian hypnotherapy, and Aikido." *American Journal of Clinical Hypnosis*, 34(4), 1992, 261-270.

Winkelman, Michael. *Shamanism: The Neural Ecology of Consciousness and Healing*. Westport, CT: Bergin and Garvey, 2000.

Winnicott, Donald W. "On the basis for self in body." In C. Winnicott, R. Shepherd & M. Davis (Eds.), *Psychoanalytic Explorations*. Cambridge, MA: Harvard University Press, (1970) 1989.

Breaking Free from the Victim Trap

Fourth printing 2004: over 30,000 books in print

This book has changed the lives of tens of thousands of readers.

It is written clearly and simply, yet carries a profound message of hope. The damage has been done, but the good news is that each of us can repair that damage.

The Victim Game is a family game taught to children in three ways.

The first is by direct example since one or more of the parents is usually a victim in families where this game is played.

Second, the child is programmed by the parent to be a victim.

Third, the victim behavior is reinforced by the parent until it becomes a permanent part of the child's identity.

The child goes through life then having one victim experience after another and each experience reinforces this person's victim position.

The Victim Game can be stopped and changed, but it takes (1) desire to change; (2) awareness; and (3) intensive therapy to change the subconscious programming.

Now, BREAKING FREE from the VICTIM TRAP
The <u>Audio</u> Program

This CD is a companion experience to the book. It is not an audio reading of the book.

Discounts for quantity purchases.

Track 1
INTRODUCTION to BREAKING FREE from the VICTIM TRAP

1. The Law of Attraction
2. Healing through Relationships
3. Addiction to the Drama
4. Reclaiming Personal Power

Track 2
HEALING *VICTIM* CONSCIOUSNESS HYPNOTHERAPY EXPERIENCE

1. Discovering Your Safe Place
2. Identifying Current **Victim** Patterns
3. Discovering the Source of the **Victim**
4. Releasing the Feelings
5. Nurturing the Inner Child
6. Creating a New Healthy Pattern
7. Empowerment Affirmations

Track 3
HEALING VICTIM CONSCIOUSNESS
***Beautiful Butterfly* (Bobbi Branch)**

Track 4
HEALING *RESCUER* CONSCIOUSNESS HYPNOTHERAPY EXPERIENCE

1. Discovering Your Safe Place
2. Identifying Current **Rescuer** Patterns
3. Discovering the Source of the **Rescuer**
4. Releasing the Feelings
5. Nurturing the Inner Child
6. Creating a New Healthy Pattern
7. Empowerment Affirmations

Track 5
HEALING RESCUER CONSCIOUSNESS
***Sing Your Own Song* (Bobbi Branch)**

Track 6
HEALING *PERSECUTOR* CONSCIOUSNESS HYPNOTHERAPY EXPERIENCE

1. Discovering Your Safe Place
2. Identifying Current **Persecutor** Patterns
3. Discovering the Source of the **Persecutor**
4. Releasing the Feelings
5. Nurturing the Inner Child
6. Creating a New Healthy Pattern
7. Empowerment Affirmations

THE WELLNESS INSTITUTE

The Chakras Meditation
2 CD set

FIRST CD
Track 1
INTRODUCTION TO MEDITATION

1. Creating Sacred Space
2. Benefits of Chakra Meditation
3. Quieting the Mind
4. Receiving a Spiritual Mantra

Track 2
ACTIVATING LOWER CHAKRAS

1. Connecting with the Earth
2. Power Animal's Message
3. Cleansing the Chakras
4. Release Energetic Drains
5. Connecting with Divine Presence

Track 3
ACTIVATING HIGHER CHAKRAS

1. Cleansing the Higher Chakras
2. Heart Space above the Head
3. Compassion for Humanity
4. Soul Retrieval
5. Aura Expansion & Healing Energy

SECOND CD
Track 1
SOUL RETRIEVAL MEDITATION

1. Discovering Soul-splits in each Chakra
2. Cleansing Soul Fragments
3. Reclaiming Soul Fragments
4. Hearing your Soul's Message
5. Embracing the Symbol in each Chakra
6. Sealing the Soul in each Chakra

Track 2
MIND - BODY - SPIRIT HEALING

1. Pranayama Breathing
2. Discovering the Glands, Hormones and Organs in each Chakra
3. Manifesting Healing in each Chakra
4. Affirmations for Mind-Body Healing
5. Focusing on specific areas for Increased Healing
6. Calling in your Healing Angels

Divine Mother and Power Animal Meditations

Track 1
CALLING IN THE DIVINE MOTHER

1. The Root Chakra - Lakshmi
2. The Sacral Chakra - Shakti
3. The Solar Plexus Chakra - Kali
4. The Heart Chakra - Durga
5. The Throat Chakra - Saraswati
6. The Third Eye Chakra - Parvati
7. The Crown Chakra – Narayani/Ishwari

Track 2
POWER ANIMAL MEDITATION

Discovering the Power Animal
in each Chakra

Finding the individual message
carried by each animal
for your healing
and personal growth

Personal Transformation Intensive
PTI

Find a PTI near you

www.PTIntensive.com

This is a profoundly healing group process, meeting for five weekend retreats over five months, in a loving environment. Do you long for these changes in your life?

Attract Healthy, Loving, Fulfilling Relationships
Belong to a new healthy, high-powered family • Develop close in-depth friendships instead of "cocktail party superficial phoniness" • Learn healthy support (not competition) • Learn to love yourself so you can love others

Experience Personal Growth and Transformation
Self-awareness • Higher consciousness • Self-discovery

Manifest Your Goals using the full power of your mind:
It's time to stop wanting things to happen in your life and time to start making things happen • Learn to use 100% of your mind to reach your full potential with a new goal-setting process • Discover your unconscious goals • Get clear on what you want • Become a member of a Master Mind Group

Improved Health with Powerful Stress Reduction Tools
Learn messages that your body is telling you • Release body hatred and shame • Relaxation Anchors • Heart-centered meditation • Conscious Breathing

Improved Finances
Prosperity and abundance principles • Master Mind groups • Learn the role of integrity in creating your abundance

Release Self -Defeating Patterns
Procrastination • "Victim, Rescuer, Persecutor" • Fear-based decisions (learn to make clear decisions) • Codependency • Unhealthy relationship patterns

Improved Communication Skills
Learn "The Clearing Process" • Stop "The Blame Game"

Take Full Responsibility for your Life!
Stop sabotaging yourself • Learn accountability and integrity • Release the shame which diminishes your self-esteem • Release self-judgment, self-blame

THE WELLNESS INSTITUTE
800-326-4418

Journal of Heart-Centered Therapies

Selected articles
APPROVED
for
Distance CE credit
(5 hours each)

APPROVALS:

Social Workers

The Wellness Institute is approved as a provider for distance continuing education by The National Association of Social Workers (NASW) to offer 5 hours of credit for each Journal article (provider # 886422919).

Professional Counselors

The Wellness Institute is recognized by the National Board of Certified Counselors to offer continuing education for certified counselors. We adhere to NBCC continuing education guidelines. Provider #5460 (5 hours of credit for each Journal article).

There are test questions and a fee of $50 per 5 hours of CE.

For complete details, call 800-326-4418, or go to:
http://www.heartcenteredtherapies.org/Journal/Distance_Learning_CEUs.htm

---

The Heart-Centered Therapies Association
3716 - 274th Ave SE, Issaquah, WA 98029 ❖ 425-391-9716 ❖ 800-326-4418

Index of Back Issues of the Journal

(all available)

The Heart-Centered Therapies Association

3716 - 274th Avenue SE, Issaquah, WA 98029 USA ❖ 425-391-9716 ❖ 800-326-4418

CLEAN BREAK
Stop Smoking Program With Hypnosis

CLEAN BREAK is a group stop-smoking program, consisting of four weekly classes. Use the power of hypnosis to help take control of unhealthy habits and replace them with new healthy ones. The hypnosis included in this program helps you become a non-smoker by accessing the subconscious where habits are formed. Each of the four weekly sessions offers a hypnosis exercise that complements the material presented in that session.

The TRIM-LIFE® Program is specifically designed to target the main problems that cause people to gain weight in the first place. The program consists of four weekly sessions and optional follow-up support sessions.

Learn how to change your blood-sugar levels and learn about nutrition, proper eating habits, and the *Hunger Level*. We target PMS-hormonal imbalance and examine *emotional eating*. Use hypnosis to release the underlying emotional need to overeat.

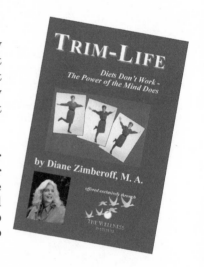

Developed by Diane Zimberoff
and offered exclusively
by The Wellness Institute

---

call 800-326-4418
to find a program provider in your area